Advertising and Competition

Advertising and Competition

by Jules Backman
Research Professor of Economics
New York University

NEW YORK • NEW YORK UNIVERSITY PRESS
LONDON • UNIVERSITY OF LONDON PRESS LIMITED

Preface

I have long had a deep interest in the operation of competition in our economy and have undertaken considerable economic research in this area. Thus, I welcomed the opportunity to study the relationship between advertising and competition afforded by a grant made available by the Association of National Advertisers. Although the original objective was to develop a pamphlet in this area, it soon became apparent that the scope of the subject was broad enough to permit the preparation of this monograph.

It has been almost an article of faith for economists to be highly critical of advertising and to decry it as wasteful of economic resources and as a source of monopoly power. Unfortunately, the criticisms have been highlighted and the small print ignored. The small print in this case usually is the proviso—"under conditions of perfect competition." In the ideal world, which economists have created for purposes of analysis, there would indeed be little or no need for advertising. But it is unfortunate when a conclusion based upon such an assumption is applied to the real world, in which the theoretical is neither attainable nor desirable. In many respects the present volume could be subtitled "An Essay in Dissent."

I wish to express my appreciation to Marvin Levine, instructor in economics, New York University, who assisted in the basic research, to Robert F. Winter, instructor in Statistics, New York University, who handled the statistical work and preparation of the charts, and to Catherine Ferfoglia, who assumed the arduous task of typing and secretarial work. Peter W. Allport, president, and William D. Kistler, vice-president of the Association of National Advertisers, provided invaluable aid in opening doors so that very useful data could be obtained. James O. Peckham, Sr., of A. C. Nielsen & Co. provided useful data compiled by that organization and critically reviewed the entire manuscript. Solomon Dutka of Audits and Survey, Inc. was also very cooperative in furnishing data. Detailed and helpful critical suggestions have also been made by Darrell B. Lucas, Professor of Marketing, New York University, Assistant Professor Charles R. Frank, Jr., of Yale University, and Martin R. Gainsbrugh, chief economist of the National Industrial Conference Board. About forty other experts in advertising also reviewed various parts of the study.

However, the conclusions and any errors of omission or commission are my sole responsibility. I would like to thank the Association of National Advertisers for making this study possible and for the fine cooperation extended by its Board of Directors and its staff.

Jules Backman

January 1967

Contents

Tables

Charts

I

Introduction

Is advertising competitive or anticompetitive? Does it provide evidence of competition or does it inhibit competition? These might seem like strange questions to the businessman, but they are posed seriously by many economists and antitrust officials. Much of the confusion arises because of the interpretations given to the meaning of competition.

The businessman has no difficulty in identifying what he considers to be competition. He knows the competitive impact of a new product or of one which is packaged more attractively or of one which is advertised more intensively and with greater imagination. He experiences the effects when a new competitor enters the market or when an existing competitor undertakes to expand its share of the market. Against this background, the businessman is understandably puzzled when he is told that these everyday experiences are not really competition because there are only a few firms in his market or because he differentiates his product in order to gain a market identity and the hoped-for loyalty of some customers or because he advertises intensively. He is surprised to find that competition often is equated solely or largely with price competition, to which many economists give primary emphasis. There has clearly been an absence of

1

communication between the two groups on this question.
Competition is a pervasive fact of economic life even
though it is difficult, or sometimes impossible, to measure
its exact extent. The late Professor John Maurice Clark has
summarized the nature of competition as follows:

> "It is the form of discipline that business units exercise
> over one another, under pressure of the discipline customers
> can exercise over the business units by virtue of their power of
> choosing between the offerings of rival suppliers. Competition
> presupposes that businesses pursue their own self-interest and
> it harnesses this force by their need of securing the customer's
> favor."[1]

> "Competition between business units in the production
> and sale of goods is the effort of such units, acting independ-
> ently of one another (without concerted action), each trying
> to make a profitable volume of sales in the face of the offers
> of other sellers of identical or closely similar products."[2]

The essence of competition is rivalry.[3] Competition
results in pressures to improve products—to "build the better
mousetraps"—and to find more economical ways to produce
and to distribute goods. The firm that fails to respond to
competitive pressures loses out to its more imaginative or
more efficient rivals. The consumer benefits by the availability of new and better products to satisfy his ever-expanding
desires. And as is shown in chapter V, many of the most
heavily advertised products have risen less in price—or
actually recorded price declines—during the postwar price
inflation.

Competition may be:

1] *offensive*—where a company initiates a change, or
2] *defensive*—where a company responds to a com-

---

1 John Maurice Clark, *Competition as a Dynamic Process,* The
Brookings Institution, Washington, D. C., 1961, p.9.

2 *Ibid.,* p. 13.

3 See A.D.H. Kaplan, *Big Enterprise in a Competitive System,* Revised Edition, The Brookings Institution, Washington, D.C., 1964, p. 44.

petitive move in order to minimize or neutralize its effect, or

3] *potential*—where other companies are "standing in the wings" ready to enter the market.

These are all dimensions of our competitive economy. When competitive moves are initiated, an effort often is made to make them distinctive in some way so that other business firms cannot meet them easily. This is why companies prefer competition through quality, warranties, delivery, credit terms, service, advertising, and other nonprice[4] means to price reductions which can be easily and quickly met by their competitors.[5] This type of competitive move gives a firm a "time advantage"—being there first with an idea and becoming identified with it—where it is difficult for a competitor to meet it promptly.

In recent years, one important facet of competition has been research and development with the accompanying flow of new and improved products and/or reductions in costs. To familiarize the public with the merits of these new and improved products often requires relatively high expenditures for promotion, including advertising.

The general public can benefit from the availability of these new and improved products in two ways. First, our rising level of living has reflected the availability for mass consumption of new products as well as the improvements in existing products. Secondly, the history of many new products has been one of declining prices[6] as demand has expanded

4 For other types of nonprice competition see Jules Backman, *Price Practices and Price Policies*, Ronald Press, New York, 1953, Ch.4, and Mark S. Massel, *Competition and Monopoly*, The Brookings Institution, Washington, D.C., 1962, pp. 3-4.

5 "Given a choice, grocery manufacturers prefer not to compete on price but rather in quality and/or other aspects of what is called 'nonprice' competition." *Studies of Organization and Competition in Grocery Manufacturing*, Technical Study No. 6, National Commission on Food Marketing, Washington, D.C., June 1966, p. 16.

6 During a period of general price inflation, these tendencies may be obscured. However, at such time an unchanged price or one that rises less than the general price level would be equivalent to a relative price decline.

and as the economies of mass production have been achieved. Advertising has contributed significantly to this development.

Although the intensely competitive nature of advertising is a matter of common observation, it has been contended that the results of large-scale advertising have been anticompetitive.[7] In effect, it is said advertising is so successful that monopolistic advantages accrue to the large advertisers. The claimed anticompetitive effects of advertising may be summarized as follows:

1] The large company has the power of the large purse, which enables it to spend substantial sums on advertising, particularly to implement varying degrees of product differentiation which enables a company to pre-empt part of a market.

2] Advertising thus creates a barrier to new firms entering an industry or a product market.

3] The result is high economic concentration.

4] Because of their protected position and because of product differentiation these firms can charge monopolistic prices which are too high. Moreover, they must recover the cost of the advertising by charging higher prices.

5] High prices in turn result in excessively large profits.

The factual basis for these claims must be evaluated. At the outset advertising should be placed in proper perspective to indicate its role in our economy. How important is advertising in the national economy? Does advertising aid economic growth? How have the various media changed in relative importance over time? What is advertising's role

7 Henry C. Simons, *Economic Policy for a Free Society,* University of Chicago Press, Chicago, Ill., 1948, p. 95, and Donald F. Turner, *Advertising and Competition,* An Address before the Briefing Conference on Federal Controls of Advertising and Promotion sponsored by the Federal Bar Association, Washington, D.C., June 2, 1966. One of the most severe indictments of advertising is contained in The Labour Party, *Report of a Commission of Enquiry Into Advertising,* (Reith Report), London, England, 1966, 205 pp.

in the "marketing mix"? What are the economic characteristics of the most heavily advertised products? Why do firms
advertise some products much more intensively than others?
Does advertising result in economic waste, that is, a misallo-
cation of resources? How significant are the tests of perfect
competition as a yardstick to judge the impact of advertising
on competition?

Do high rates of advertising lead to economic concentration or create barriers to entry? What has happened to relative
market shares of firms selling heavily advertised products?
What has been the experience with nationally advertised
brands? Have heavily advertised products risen more in price
than less-advertised items during the post-World War II
price inflation? Have high advertising expenditures been so
successful in creating a monopoly position that they have
resulted in very high profit rates?

These are some of the questions which are analyzed in
the following chapters to determine the relationship between
advertising and competition.

II

Advertising in Perspective

The competitive impact of advertising cannot be examined in a vacuum. It must be viewed against the background of an economy which has been experiencing an explosive growth and within a framework of alternative selling tools. In the past generation, this nation's level of living has doubled, thereby providing a highly favorable environment for an expanded volume of advertising. During the same period general price inflation has resulted in a marked rise in the price level, including the cost of advertising. Thus, the increase in advertising expenditures reflects an amalgam of forces, only one of which is the intensification of competition for the consumer's dollar.

To place advertising in proper perspective a number of questions must be answered. To what extent does the rise in the dollar volume of advertising reflect the general price inflation prevalent in our postwar economy? Have real advertising expenditures risen more rapidly than the output of the economy? How has the "mix" among media been affected by the development of television? What are the economic characteristics of highly advertised products? What is the relationship between advertising and economic growth? How has the postwar proliferation of new products affected the level of advertising expenditures? Does advertising influence significantly the level of the total demand for goods and services or are other forces of greater importance?

Although advertising plays a key role in the marketing programs for many products, it is only one part of that program and hence must be evaluated in relationship to other phases of marketing. What alternatives are available to advertising? Does advertising increase the total cost of marketing? How does the "marketing mix" vary for different sectors of the economy? How important in the consumer's budget are heavily advertised products?

Other questions must be considered in connection with the evaluation given to the role of advertising by economists. Does advertising represent economic waste? What is the magnitude of national advertising against which the charge of economic waste is most often directed? How would demand for new products, which contributes so much to economic growth, be developed without large-scale promotion, including advertising? What are the prerequisites for perfect competition, the yardstick often used by economists to measure the usefulness of advertising? Is this a meaningful yardstick in the real world?

Of course, it is easier to pose such questions than to answer them satisfactorily. In this chapter, the available materials are reviewed as they bear upon these questions.

Trend of Dollar Advertising Expenditures

In the pre-World War II period, total advertising expenditures averaged about $2.0 billion. By the end of the war the total had increased to $2.9 billion. During the postwar period, expenditures for advertising have risen virtually without interruption.[1] The total reached $5 billion in 1949, $10 billion in 1957, and $15 billion in 1965. (For the basic data

1 Reductions of less than 1% occurred in 1958 and 1961; there were mild contractions in economic activity in these years.

and their limitations, see Appendix Table A-1) Thus, advertising expenditures doubled in the eight-year period 1949 to 1957 but increased by only 50% in the following eight years.

How the favorable postwar economic environment stimulated advertising expenditures is evident by their relationship to key measures of national economic activity. Total advertising expenditures responded to the rapid growth of our national economy. Chart II-1 relates the total annual expenditures for advertising as published by *Printers' Ink* to personal consumption expenditures.[2] As the economy has expanded, expenditures for advertising have followed a similar course.

Although cause-and-effect relationships are difficult to disentangle, it seems far more probable that the rise in economic activity has caused the rise in advertising rather than the reverse. But advertising was also causative of economic growth as well as its beneficiary. The postwar period has seen a flood of new products moving into mass consumption. To the extent that advertising has facilitated the development and acceptance of these products, it has contributed most constructively to economic growth.

Trend of Real Advertising Expenditures

The significance of this sharp rise in advertising expenditures should not be viewed as a detached phenomenon. It developed over a quarter of a century, characterized by a substantial amount of price inflation.[3] All broad measures of economic activity in terms of dollars have reflected this

2 The line of relationship shown on the chart is based on 30 years of experience from 1935 to 1965. For the statistical relationships with other national aggregates and for measures of statistical significance see Appendix A.

3 The consumer price index increased by 125%, the wholesale price index by 138%, and the implicit price index by 153% between 1940 and 1965. For an analysis of the significance of each of these indexes as measures of price inflation see Jules Backman and Martin R. Gainsbrugh, *Inflation and the Price Indexes,* Joint Economic Committee, Congress of the United States, 89th Cong., 2nd Sess., Washington, D.C., July 1966.

CHART II-1

Relationship between Advertising and
Personal-Consumption Expenditures, 1935-1965

Advertising
Expenditures
in Billions
of Dollars

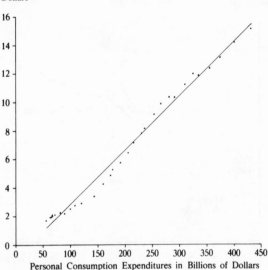

Personal Consumption Expenditures in Billions of Dollars

inflationary surge.[4]

The price of advertising has not been exempt from these general inflationary pressures. An implicit advertising cost index[5] has been calculated for the post-World War II period. (See Appendix B.) Between 1946 and 1965, the implicit advertising cost index rose by 46.7% as compared with 55.1% in the total wholesale price index and 61.6% in the consumer

4 For example, personal consumption expenditures in current dollars increased more than 500% between 1940 and 1965. The real increase, when the effects of price inflation are eliminated, was only 154%. Between 1946 and 1965, the increases were 200% and 95% respectively. Derived from the *Economic Report of the President,* January 1967, pp. 213-14.

5 This index was derived by comparing the actual dollars spent on

CHART II-2

Wholesale and Consumer Price Indexes, 1939-1965, and the Implicit Advertising Cost Index, 1946 and 1950-1965

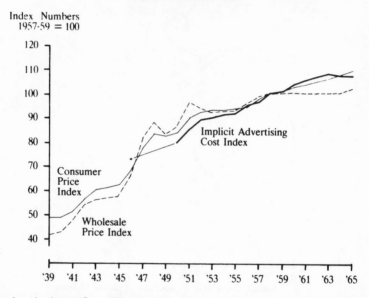

price index. (See Chart II-2) Part of the rise in advertising costs after 1946 represented a "catch up" for the lag which developed in the 1940-1946 period.[6]

After eliminating the price factor, the increase in real

media advertising with the aggregate number of real dollars (actual dollars for each medium adjusted by the rate changes for that medium). As is pointed out in Appendix B the index may *understate* the actual rise in advertising costs to the extent that the television component recorded a smaller decline or a rise in contrast to the decline recorded in the *Printers' Ink* series.

6 The milline rate for newspapers *decreased* by 3.0% from 1940 to 1946 and magazine rates per 1000 circulation *decreased* by 2.9%. Third-class postage rates remained unchanged during this period. From 1940 to 1946 the WPI rose 53.7% and the CPI 39.3%.

advertising expenditures was 212% from 1946 to 1965.[7] This is much smaller than the increase of 357% in actual dollars but it still represents a substantial rise. (See Chart II-3.)

CHART II-3

Indexes of Advertising Expenditures, 1946, 1950-1965 in Constant and Current Dollars

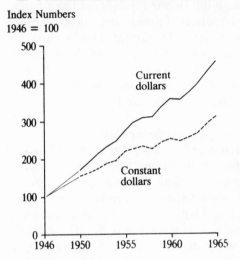

Index Numbers
1946 = 100

Changing Shares by Media

The sharp expansion in the dollar volume of advertising has been shared by all major media[8]—but to different degrees. This fact may be overlooked sometimes when attention is focused on the dramatic growth of television in the past fifteen years and on the disappearance of many newspapers[9] and some national magazines.

7 If the implicit index understates the rise in advertising costs because of the television component, the increase in real advertising expenditures is somewhat overstated.

8 For a discussion of the advantages of each medium see Darrell B. Lucas and Steuart H. Britt, *Measuring Advertising Effectiveness,* McGraw-Hill Book Co., Inc., New York, 1963, Ch. 9.

9 For example, the total number of *daily* newspapers declined from

Newspapers have been by far the major outlet for advertising expenditures. During the past quarter of a century, the increase in the total volume of newspaper advertising was $3.6 billion as compared with $2.5 billion for television![10] This sharp dollar rise in newspaper advertising reflects the heavy utilization of this medium by local advertisers, particularly the retail trade![11]

Although the dollar totals have risen for all media, the relative distribution of these expenditures among the several media has changed markedly. (See Charts II-4 and II-5.) Television has carved its relative share largely out of the proportion formerly going to newspapers and radio and to some extent out of that formerly obtained by magazines. (See Appendix Tables A-7 and A-8)

Factors Affecting Consumer Demand

The demand for any product is influenced by a wide variety of factors including: levels and changes in consumer incomes, prices, availability and cost of substitute products, changes in population, geography, tastes, religion, and customs, as well as advertising. However, it is not always possible to determine which factor is most significant for each product.

The total demand for all consumer goods is most significantly influenced by total disposable personal income. Total retail sales are closely correlated to broad changes in consumer incomes after taxes![12] However, as incomes rise, the

---

1,878 in 1940 to 1,763 in 1964 but their circulation rose from 41.1 million to 60.4 million. The total number of newspapers (includes daily, weekly, semi-weekly, and Sunday) declined from 10,282 in 1947 to 8,645 in 1958, U.S. Department of Commerce, Bureau of the Census, *Statistical Abstract of the United States: 1965,* Washington, D.C., 1965, pp. 524-25.

10 Since 1949, the first year for which we have data for television advertising, the total in newspapers increased by $2,541 million and for television by $2,466 million.

11 In 1940 and in 1965, local advertising accounted for about 80% of the total in newspapers.

12 *Survey of Current Business,* May 1961, p. 26 and April 1962, p.19.

pattern of spending changes gradually, with a smaller percentage used to buy foods and other necessities. The proportion spent for foods declined from 26.0% in 1950 to 21.0% in 1965,[13] despite the shift to more expensive convenience foods. In contrast, medical care expenditures increased from 4.2% of disposable personal income in 1950 to 6.0% in 1965. Private education increased from 0.8% to 1.2%. The year-to-year changes usually have been very small because spending patterns are relatively fixed and are not changed easily.

Within an industry there may be changes in shares obtained by companies or for particular brands, as will be noted later, but the over-all share of the consumer's dollar obtained by an industry changes only gradually. Advertising helps to influence these changes in shares and to expand total demand to some extent, particularly when new or improved products are made available. But advertising is not the prime deter-

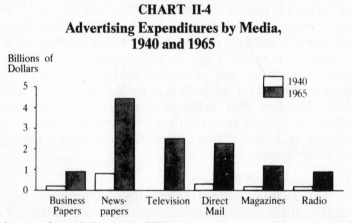

CHART II-4
Advertising Expenditures by Media,
1940 and 1965

minant of total demand. When incomes are rising, there is also an increased opportunity to utilize advertising effectively.

Importance of Largest Advertisers

In 1965, the 125 largest national advertisers each spent

13 These data reflect changes in prices and in volume.

CHART II-5

Major Media Shares of Total Advertising Expenditures, 1940, 1950, and 1965

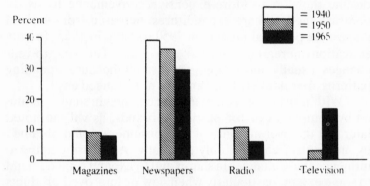

$7.9 million or more. This total includes expenditures for the eight measured media. They are estimated to have spent $4.1 billion on all types of advertising or 26.7% of the total.[14] The top 5 companies each spent more than $100 million, 6 spent between $75 and $100 million, 10 spent between $50 and $75 million. In contrast, close to three-quarters of all advertising expenditures was accounted for by companies which spent less than $7.9 million a year for this purpose. It seems clear, therefore, that although there are some companies which are very large users of advertising, the bulk of the advertising dollars is spent by smaller advertisers throughout American industry.

Highly Advertised Products

One useful measure of the intensity of advertising expenditures is their relationship to sales. Absolute dollar totals alone are important but do not tell the story of intensity. An analysis[15] of the percent of advertising to total sales for the 125 largest advertisers in 1965 showed that of 32 companies which spent 10% or more of their sales dollar on advertising:

14 For national media, expenditures for the 125 companies were $2.9 billion or 33.0% of the total.

15 *Advertising Age,* August 29, 1966. p. 44.

17 companies sold drugs and cosmetics
4 companies sold soaps and cleaners
3 companies sold soft drinks
2 companies sold gum and candies
6 were in other industries

In other words, the biggest relative users of advertising are concentrated in 5 industries—drugs, cosmetics, soaps, soft drinks, and gum and candies. Among the products for which large advertisers spent between 5% and 10% of the sales dollar for advertising were cigarettes, many foods, liquor, and beer.[16] The economic characteristics of these industries and the intensely competitive attitudes of the constituent companies explain why these large advertising expenditures are made. Moreover, the extensive product differentiation which characterizes these industries is accompanied by large-scale advertising.

Except for liquor, some drugs,[17] and some cosmetics, these products usually sell for less than $1 a unit and in many instances for less than 50 cents. They are relatively low-priced items which are available from many retail establishments. They are subject to frequent repeat purchases[18] so that the consumer is able to check performance against claims very readily as well as to test out rival claims. The consumer also is willing to experiment with new brands.[19] These are brutally competitive markets in which old brands die and new products and new brands are made available frequently.

16 In contrast, advertising costs tended to average less than 2% of total sales for cars, tires, oil, appliances, chemicals, and metals; for airlines, paper products, and photographic equipment they average between 2% and 5%.

17 16 out of 24 proprietary drugs shown in Appendix Table E-8 sold for less than $1 in 1966.

18 It has been reported that "the typical consumer" buys soap or detergent 50 times a year, toothpaste 11 times, coffee 22 times. The Procter & Gamble Company, *Annual Report For Year Ended June 30, 1966,* p. 6.

19 Lester G. Telser, "Supply and Demand For Advertising Messages," *American Economic Review, Papers and Proceedings,* May 1966, pp. 463-66.

As a result, market shares for any product may change sharply and dramatically.

Many of the products may be differentiated in some way from competing products even though functionally they may be substitutable. Differentiated products usually have brands so that the product may be easily identified by the consumer. This places a premium on quality, since the consumer can readily blame—or give credit—to the manufacturer.[20] Of course, the existence of a brand does not assure demand by consumers. As in all sectors of our economy, the demand for products covered by some brands may be expanding while in other instances it may be stable or contracting.

Joe S. Bain has defined a "significantly . . . substantial level" of advertising as 5% or more of sales and a "rather low . . . level" as below 2% of sales revenue.[21] However, there is no way to determine what percentage represents a significant cutoff point for "high" or "low" advertising. The situation in each industry must be evaluated separately.[22] For example, an industry with many new products and/or many new brands would normally have greater recourse to advertising than industries in which product lines are more stable. Similarly, the proportion of a company's sales derived from sales to government agencies or to industrial purchases affects the significance of advertising as a percentage of a company's total sales. Only by analyzing the varying economic characteristics of the products involved can we understand

20 Borden has emphasized so-called "hidden qualities" and pointed out that "When these hidden qualities are present, consumers tend to rely upon the brand and advertising can be used to associate the presence of the qualities with the brand." Neil H. Borden, *The Economic Effects of Advertising,* Richard D. Irwin, Inc., Chicago, Ill., 1942, p. 425.

21 Joe S. Bain, *Industrial Organization,* John Wiley & Sons, Inc., New York, 1959, pp. 390-91. The Reith Report also defined "substantially advertised products" at 5% or more. *op. cit.,* p. 42.

22 It should be kept in mind that the dollar expenditure required to purchase exposure in a given medium is the same whether the advertiser has a large volume of sales or a low volume. The relationship of advertising cost to sales, however, could differ significantly.

the reasons for the diverse intensities which have developed in the use of advertising.

Advertising in the "Marketing Mix"

Advertising is only one selling tool; it is part of a broad marketing process. There are other techniques available—and widely used—to build up sales. These include product planning, pricing, varying channels of distribution, personal selling, promotions, packaging, display materials, and servicing.[23] For some products, direct selling is important, while for others large amounts may be spent to market through wholesalers or brokers. Food stores have used the inducement of stamp plans, and participated in prize contests, free samples, and price-off coupons.[24] Often these techniques are complementary rather than substitutable. The combinations selected usually are at the option of the company, although competitive pressures may result in greater emphasis upon some of the alternatives available.

Advertising may play widely varying roles in the marketing mix for different products. Thus, marketing costs for breakfast cereals and for crackers and cookies were similar in 1964, 27.0% and 24.3% of sales respectively. Yet, for breakfast cereals advertising accounted for 14.9% while for crackers and cookies the proportion was only 2.2%.[25] (See Chart II-6)

23 Neil H. Borden, "The Concept of the Marketing Mix" in *Science In Marketing*, edited by George Schwartz, John Wiley & Sons, Inc., New York, 1965, pp. 389-90.

24 It has been estimated that soap manufacturers spent $250 million on advertising and an additional $150 million on other types of sales promotion. Spencer Klaw, "The Soap Wars: A Strategic Analysis," *Fortune*, June 1963, p. 123. Procter and Gamble was reported to have 1,800 salesmen. *Procter and Gamble v. FTC*, U.S. Circuit Court of Appeals for the Sixth District, March 18, 1966 (Commerce Clearing House, *Federal Regulation Reports*, Volume 5, March 24, 1966, p. 82 182). Coffee roasters spent an estimated $53.2 million on advertising and "about $100 million on price promotion deals" in 1965. Ted Sanchagrin, "Coffee: Ad Volume and Consumption Dip," *Printers' Ink*, August 12, 1966, p. 28.

25 "Grocery Manufacturing," *op. cit.*, p. 147. A study of marketing costs in 66 consumer goods industries showed that in 1956, 25 spent more

CHART II-6
Marketing Costs as a Percent of Sales, 1964

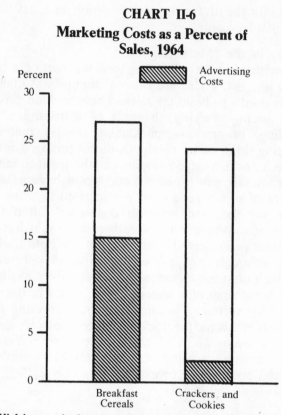

Within an industry, the mix also may vary widely as companies follow different marketing strategies. Thus, although the cosmetics industry has been estimated to spend about 15% of its sales on advertising, Avon spends only 2.7% on advertising because it sells on a house-to-house basis.[26] Yet it has been a highly successful company.[27]

Within a company, too, the marketing mix may differ

---

on advertising than on other marketing costs, 5 spent equal amounts, and 36 spent less on advertising. Dale Houghton, "Marketing Costs: What Ratio to Sales?" *Printers' Ink,* February 1, 1957, pp. 54-55.

26 Penelope Orth, "Cosmetics: The Brand Is Everything," *Printers' Ink,* November 1, 1963, p. 30.

27 In 1965, Avon reported total sales of $352 million which made it

Marketing Component	Percent of Sales, 1964 Breakfast Cereals	Crackers and Cookies
Personal selling	2.0	7.9
Advertising	14.9	2.2
Sales promotion	2.1	2.0
Marketing research	0.5	0.1
Research and development	2.3	0.4
Physical distribution	5.2	11.7
Total	27.0	24.3

among products. Data available for The Procter & Gamble Company of Canada, Limited are illustrative. For toilet soaps, the company spent 13.5% of gross sales for advertising (direct and cooperative) and 5.5% for sales promotion in 1966 while for cake mixes the ratios were 8.2% and 7.5% respectively and for packaged detergents 11.3% and 6.9%; for bulk detergents, sales promotion cost 0.8%, and there was no advertising.[28]

It has been reported that "One grocery manufacturer does not use media advertising at all, but spends a large sum on trade allowances and incentives. The company's marketing expenditures, as a percent of sales, are comparable to those of another manufacturer which places strong reliance on consumer advertising."[29] In such a situation, the company which elects *not* to advertise effects no reduction in total marketing costs.

McGraw-Hill made a study of the relative importance of total marketing costs and of advertising costs of 227 industrial companies which were selling to other businesses. It showed that such industrial advertising *and* sales promotion expenses were 2.2% of sales in 1963 as compared with total marketing costs (including direct selling, operating costs of advertising and sales departments, and warehouse and

192 in rank among the 500 largest industrial companies. In terms of profit as a percent of invested capital, it ranked second. *Fortune,* July 1966, pp. 238-39.

28 Submission to the Special Joint Committee of the Senate and House of Commons on Food Prices, Canada, December 1, 1966, Appendix 3.

29 "Grocery Manufacturing," *op. cit.,* p. 17.

delivery) of 15.1%. The experience by industries was as follows:[30]

Industry	Percent of Total Sales	
	Total Marketing Costs	Advertising and Sales Promotion
Rubber and plastic	13.1	1.5
Stone, clay, and glass	13.2	1.8
Fabricated metal	16.6	3.0
Machinery except electrical	15.6	2.2
Electrical machinery and supplies	15.6	2.4
Instruments, photographic and optical goods	15.6	2.1
All others	13.4	1.6
TOTAL	15.1	2.2

For these industrial companies, advertising and sales promotion expense accounted for only about one-seventh of the total marketing costs, since advertising plays a different role for industrial products than for consumer goods. The aim of much industrial advertising is to make the salesman's task easier to complete, thus making possible more calls and a more effective performance.

Advertising may make it possible to hold down other marketing costs so that the expenditures for advertising do not represent entirely a net increase in total expenditures for marketing. For example, the considerable success of discount houses, vending machines, and self-service stores[31] has been accompanied by reduced personal selling costs and is undoubtedly due in part to the fact that the consumer

30 *Industrial Marketing Costs*—1963, McGraw-Hill, June 1964. See also *How Advertising Affects the Cost of Selling,* McGraw-Hill, July 1963, passim.

31 *Fortune* reported that "... the rise of the self-service store has caused soap manufacturers to cut back on promotional efforts aimed at store-keepers, and to concentrate even more single-mindedly than in the past on selling the consumer directly." June 1963, pp. 182, 184. However, Borden reported that "frequently the use of advertising does not bring a reduction in personal selling costs or total marketing costs." Borden, *op. cit.,* p. xxxi.

has been made aware through advertising of the alternatives available. Not only does this mean a reduction in personal selling costs to distributors but it also reduces his promotional costs since they are borne mainly by the manufacturer.[32] According to Dr. David M. Blank, the result has been a " . . . considerable growth in efficiency in distribution, an economic sector that has traditionally lagged behind goods-producing industries in gains in productivity." [33]

The Harvard Business Review conducted an extensive survey of advertising in 1962 and reported:

> What would happen if advertising expenditures were eliminated? Would other selling expenses take their place? *Definitely yes,* reply businessmen. Over 85% believe that other selling expenses would take advertising's place if advertising were eliminated, with only 10% disagreeing. This finding holds generally true irrespective of management level, industry, or function.[34]

Actually, the real problem for any firm is to determine the best "marketing mix" in which advertising is but one ingredient.[35]

Advertising and Economic Growth

Economic growth has become a major objective of national economic policy in recent years. Rising productivity, increasing population, improving education, rates of saving, and decisions concerning new investments are

32 Committee on Advertising, *Principles of Advertising,* Pitman Publishing Corp., New York, 1963, p. 29.

33 David M. Blank, "Some Comments On The Role of Advertising in the American Economy—A Plea For Revaluation," in *Reflections On Progress in Marketing,* edited by L. George Smith, Northern Illinois University, 1964 Educators Conference, American Marketing Association, Chicago, Illinois, 1964, p. 152.

34 Stephen A. Greyser, "Businessmen Re Advertising: Yes, But . . . ," *Harvard Business Review,* May-June 1962, p. 30.

35 Walter Taplin, "Advertising Appropriation Policy," *Economica,* August 1959, pp. 229-30.

the ingredients of economic growth. In addition, there must be a favorable political climate including tax policies and monetary policies designed to release the forces conducive to growth.[36]

Advertising contributes to economic growth by complementing the efforts to create new and improved products through expenditures for research and development.[37]   One observer has described the process as follows:

" . . . advertising, by acquainting the consumer with the values of new products, widens the market for these products, pushes forward their acceptance by the consumer and encourages the investment and entrepreneurship necessary for innovation. Advertising, in short, holds out the promise of a greater and speedier return than would occur without such methods, thus stimulating investment, growth, and diversity."[38]

Former Secretary of Commerce, Luther Hodges noted that: "Without advertising's ability to stimulate the constantly expanding demand for goods and services, our gross national product would not have more than doubled in the past 20 years."[39]

36 Jules Backman and Martin R. Gainsbrugh, *The Forces Influencing the American Economy,* New York University School of Commerce, New York, 1965; Edward F. Denison, *The Sources of Economic Growth in the United States and the Alternatives Before Us,* Supplementary Paper No. 13, Committee for Economic Development, New York, January, 1962.

37 Secretary of the Treasury Henry H. Fowler has noted that advertising encourages research and development. "Advertising plays a key role . . . in the function and growth of the whole economy . . . Advertising brings us the news that something new and better has been made." *Responsible Conduct and the American Economy Today and Ten Years From Now,* An Address before the Television Bureau of Advertising, Inc., Chicago, Ill., November 16, 1966 (mimeo), pp. 2-3.

38 Blank, *op. cit.,* p. 151. See also Neil H. Borden, "The Role of Advertising in Various Stages of Corporate and Economic Growth" in *Marketing and Economic Development,* edited by Peter D. Bennett, 1965 Fall Conference, The Pennsylvania State University, American Marketing Association, Chicago, Illinois, 1965, p. 495.

39 House Committee on Interstate and Foreign Commerce, *Hearings*

During the postwar years, there has been an explosive growth in spending for industrial research and development. American industry spent $1.1 billion for this purpose in 1946 and $13.8 billion in 1965; part of this total was financed by government. (See Table II-1)

Table II-1

Research and Development Expenditures, Selected Years, 1946-65

	Financed By Industry	Financed By Government (millions)	Total
1946	N.A.	N.A.	$1,050
1951	N.A.	N.A.	2,150
1955	$2,180	$2,180	4,640
1960	4,430	4,430	10,510
1963	5,380	5,380	12,720
1965	N.A.	N.A.	13,825

N.A. Not Available
Source: National Science Foundation and McGraw-Hill

One result has been a steady flow of new products (e.g., color TV, diet drinks, electric toothbrushes, filter cigarettes, instant tea) and new processes (e.g., stay press, spray cans), and changes in old products (e.g., color phones, photography, margarine, detergents, deodorants).[40] If such products are to move in volume from the laboratory to the marketplace, potential customers must learn about them. Advertising plays the key role in this informational process. Without it the profit incentive to engage in research and development for consumer goods would be significantly impaired. This is why Milton C. Mumford, chairman of the Board of Lever Brothers, has identified advertising

---

on Fair Packaging and Labeling, Part 2, 89th Congress, 2nd Session, Washington, D.C., 1966, p. 1094.

40 It must be recognized that some product changes have been criticized as being trivial and intended to provide a new "talking point" for purposes of advertising rather than yielding any significant benefits to the customer (e.g. tailfins for automobiles).

as "the prime mover behind product improvement and new product innovation."[41]

Among the most intensive advertisers have been toilet preparations, (14.7% of sales), cleaning and polishing preparations (12.6%), and drugs (9.4%). The markets for these products have been expanding much more rapidly than all consumer spending.[42] (See Chart II-7 and Appendix Table E-1.)

The increases in relative importance are based upon dollar totals. However, the retail prices of these products rose less than the consumer price index during the postwar years. (See Appendix Table C-2). Thus, the increase in relative importance of these highly advertised products has been even greater in real terms.

Clearly, the advertising for these products has not been entirely a "puss-in-the-corner game"[43] for the available business. Rather, it has been a significant force which contributed to an expansion in the demand for these products and to the growth of our economy with the accompanying expansion in job opportunities and in economic well-being.

Advertising of New Products

Advertising expenditures usually are significantly greater when a new product is launched than for an established product. Companies must inform potential customers about new products to build up the market for them. Through advertising and related selling efforts, producers seek to increase the willingness of consumers to use part of their expanding incomes to buy these new and improved products.

41 Milton C. Mumford, "The Advertising Agency as a Business Institution," An Address Before the AAAA meeting, Scottsdale, Arizona, April 30, 1966, p. 15.

42 For example, it has been reported that in 1966 "there were 268 men's colognes or twice as many as in 1963.""Male Call," *Sales Management,* October 15, 1966, p. 111.

43 Otto Kleppner, *Advertising Procedure,* Fifth Edition, Prentice-Hall, Inc., Englewood Cliffs, N. J., 1966, pp. 543-45; Mr. Kleppner lists a number of dramatic changes in market demand.

CHART II-7

Changes in Relative Importance of Selected Personal Consumption Expenditures, 1940, 1950, 1960, and 1965

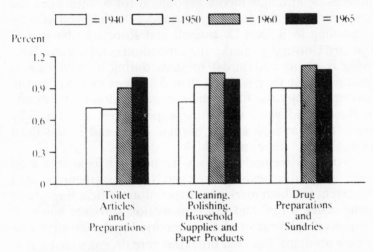

As compared with existing products, advertising costs for a new product tend to be a very high proportion of total sales during the first one or two years it is on the market.[44] Studies by A. C. Nielsen & Co. have shown that for a new toilet-good product to be successful it must "over a twenty-four month period . . . produce a share of advertising about one and one-half times that of the share of sales" sought.[45] Thus, a product seeking to obtain a 10% share of a market must

44 This is due in part to the time it takes to build up sales volume. See Telser, *op. cit.,* p. 463.

45 James O. Peckham, "Formula For Marketing New Brands of Toilet Goods," An Address before the Toilet Goods Association, Dixville Notch, New Hampshire, June 27, 1964, p. 10. An even higher proportion of advertising was found to be necessary for grocery products. James O. Peckham, "Recipe For Marketing," An Address before the Grocery Manufacturers of America, Inc., New York City, November 12, 1963, p. 15. See also David K. Hardin, "Allocating the Marketing Dollar Through Research," An Address before the Association of National Advertisers, Colorado Springs, Colo., October 24, 1966, pp. 6-7 and Exhibit 1.

have a volume of advertising equal to about 15% of the total spent in advertising those products.

Another A. C. Nielsen study showed that for 14 brands of new cold cereals introduced from 1957 to August 1, 1961, advertising in major media accounted for 47% of sales the first year, 22% the second year, and 21% the third year.[46] According to Robert D. Buzzell and Robert E. Nourse of Harvard University "marketing expenditures (of which advertising is about two-thirds) to sales during a [cold cereal] product's first year is more than 3½ times as great as the corresponding ratio for cereal companies' total operations; in the second year, marketing expenditures are typically about twice as high as the 'normal' level; and in the third year, about 1½ times normal."[47]

An intensive study of product innovation for several food processing industries by Buzzell and Nourse has demonstrated the extent to which marketing expenditures, including advertising, sales force, and sales promotion (product samples, coupons, display materials) are increased by the development of new products. For cold breakfast cereals, cake mixes, dog food, frozen dinners and specialties, margarine, and other categories of products, the weighted average ratio of mar-

Marketing Costs As Per Cent of Sales [48]

	First Year	Second Year
Cold breakfast cereals	66	30
Cake mixes	67	70
Dog food	70	N.A.
Frozen dinners and specialties	31	N.A.
Margarine	53	36
All categories	57	37

46 Cited in "Grocery Manufacturing," op. cit., p. 152.

47 Robert D. Buzzell and Robert E. Nourse, *Product Innovation, the Product Life Cycle and Competitive Behavior in Selected Food Processing Industries, 1947-64,* Arthur D. Little, Inc., Cambridge, Mass., 1966, p. 48.

48 *Ibid.,* p. 98. The data for "all categories" include additional products for which separate data were not available.

keting expenditures to total sales of new products averaged 57% during the first year and 37% in the second year.

The average ratio for new products was 4.1 times the company average in the first year and 2.4 times the company average in the second year.[49] The authors of the study concluded that the increase in the relative importance of new products "... undoubtedly is one of the causes of the increase which has, in fact, taken place in marketing expenditures. The average marketing/sales ratio [for 17 companies] increased from 12.4 percent to 14.4 percent ... It seems clear ... that innovation was a major factor contributing to the upward trend in marketing expenditures."[50] Unfortunately, separate data for advertising expenditures were not shown.

For companies or industries in which large numbers of new or modified products are brought to the market annually, total marketing costs including advertising costs would tend to be relatively higher than for companies which sell products subject to less frequent changes. Since competitive pressures play a key role in the introduction of these new brands, with the accompanying higher advertising costs, the latter are an integral part of the competitive process.

Relative Importance in Consumer's Budget

How important in the consumer's budget are the products which have been characterized as having a "significantly substantial" level of advertising? The weights assigned to

Products	Advertising as Percent of Sales, 1962 (percent)	Weights in Consumer Price Index December 1963
Toilet preparations	14.72	1.52
Soaps	12.55	.26
Drugs	9.39	.50*
Beer and malt	6.89	1.06
Tobacco	5.28	1.74
TOTAL		5.08

*Proprietary Drugs

49 Buzzell and Nourse, *op. cit.*, p. 98.
50 *Ibid.*, pp. 100-1.

these categories of products in the consumer price index are shown above.

Not all the products included in these groups have expenditures in excess of 5% of sales for advertising, and hence the aggregate ratio of 5.08% probably is on the high side. On the other hand, the tabulation does not include several products for which the ratio was above 5% but for which the industrywide average sales ratio was less than 5%. Included in this category, with the weights assigned to the entire group in the consumer price index are: cereals (.20%), soft drinks (.15%), candy (.16%), and some liquors (.78%). Probably a reasonable estimate is that between 5% and 6% of the total expenditures of a moderate-income family are for products subject to relatively large advertising expenditures.[51]

Waste in Advertising

Despite its important informational role, advertising often is criticized as being wasteful[52] because of (a) competition in advertising and (b) inefficiency in the use of advertising. Critics have directed their fire largely at competition in advertising. However, there is widespread recognition

---

51 As measured by their share of total personal consumption expenditures as reported by the U.S. Department of Commerce, the available data show: toilet articles and preparations 1.0%, cleaning and polishing preparations, miscellaneous household supplies and paper products, 1.0%, tobacco products (includes cigars) 2.0%, and drug preparations and sundries 1.1% of which 0.3% may be estimated to be over-the-counter proprietary drug products. *Survey of Current Business,* July 1966, p. 20.

52 Kenneth E. Boulding, *Economic Analysis,* Vol. 1, Microeconomics, 4th Edition, Harper & Row, New York, 1966, pp. 513-14; Nicholas H. Kaldor "The Economic Aspects of Advertising," *The Review of Economic Studies,* 1950-1951, No. 45, p. 6; George Leland Bach, *Economics,* Fifth Edition, Prentice-Hall, Inc., Englewood Cliffs, N.J., 1966, pp.431-39; Stuart Chase, *The Tragedy of Waste,* Macmillan Co., New York, 1928, p. 112; Richard Caves, *American Industry: Structure, Conduct, Performance,* Prentice-Hall, Inc., Englewood Cliffs, N.J., 1964, p. 102; "Food From Farmer To Consumer," *op. cit.,* p. 100; Campbell R. McConnell, *Economics: Principles, Problems, and Policies,* Third Edition, McGraw-Hill, Inc., New York, 1966, pp. 512-13.

that inefficiences may develop in advertising as in other phases of business[53] Mistakes undoubtedly are made in determining how much should be spent for advertising— but these mistakes can result in spending too little as well as too much.

Sometimes it is claimed that all advertising is wasteful or that the resources devoted to advertising can better be devoted to other purposes[54] Such an extreme and undiscriminating condemnation of all advertising ignores some pertinent facts.

As Professor George J. Stigler of the University of Chicago has stated:

> . . . Under competition, the main tasks of a seller are to inform potential buyers of his existence, his line of goods, and his prices. Since both sellers and buyers change over time (due to birth, death, migration), since people forget information once acquired, and since new products appear, the existence of sellers must be continually advertised . . . This informational function of advertising must be emphasized because of a popular and erroneous belief that advertising consists chiefly of nonrational (emotional and repetitive) appeals. Even the seller of aluminum ingots or 2,000 horse-power engines advertises (and makes extensive use of solicitation through salesmen), although he is dealing only with more or less hard-headed business men[55]

Elsewhere, Professor Stigler has pointed out that " . . . information is a valuable resource," that advertising is "the

53 See, for example, "Committee on Advertising," *op. cit.,* p. 34 and Borden, "The Role of Advertising in the Various Stages of Corporate and Economic Growth,"*op. cit.,* p. 493.

54 Professor Bach states: "Over-all, it is difficult for anyone to gain more than temporarily from large advertising outlays in an economy in which counteradvertising is general. The over-all effect of advertising, on which we spent $14 billion [actually $15 billion—JB] in 1965, is to devote these productive resources (men, ink, billboards, and so forth) to producing advertising rather than to producing other goods and services." Bach, *op. cit.,* p. 437.

55 George J. Stigler, *The Theory of Price,* Third Edition, The Macmillan Company, New York, 1966, p. 200.

obvious method of identifying buyers and sellers" which "reduces drastically the cost of search," and that "It is clearly an
immensely powerful instrument for the elimination of
ignorance . . ." [56]

In 1965, total expenditures for media advertising (in-
cluding direct mail) aggregated $12.3 billion. It is impossible
to determine exactly how much of this amount was strictly
informational. However, the following facts are of interest:
Classified advertising was $1.2 billion.
Other local newspaper advertising,
     largely retail, was $2.4 billion.
Business-paper advertising was $671 million.
Local radio and local TV advertising was $1.0 billion.
Spot radio and spot TV advertising was $1.1 billion.
National advertising on network TV, network
     radio, magazines, and newspapers was $3.4 billion.
Direct mail was $2.3 billion.

Classified advertising and local advertising are primarily
informational in nature. Certainly some part of national
advertising also performs this function. These figures suggest
that substantially less than half of total media advertising is of
the type that the critics are attacking as wasteful;[57] the exact
amount cannot be pinpointed.[58]

Moreover, it must be kept in mind that advertising does
more than inform. In the words of John W. Hobson:

> . . . Advertising is a service of suggestions; more than
> information, a little less than persuasion; sometimes intro-
> ducing new variants of existing satisfactions, sometimes
> evoking latent wants that people had not realised they can

56 George J. Stigler, "The Economics of Information," *The Journal
of Political Economy,* June 1961, pp. 213, 216, 220. See also S.A. Ozga,
"Imperfect Markets Through Lack of Knowledge," *Quarterly Journal of
Economics,* Feb. 1960, pp. 29, 33-4, and Wroe Alderson, *Dynamic Market
Behavior,* Richard D. Irwin, Inc., Homewood, Ill., 1965, pp. 128, 131.

57 For the United Kingdom, the "disputed proportion" of advertising
expenditures has been estimated at about 30% of the total. Walter Taplin,
Advertising, A New Approach, Little, Brown & Co., Boston, Mass., 1963,
p. 126.

58 From another point of view, even if there is waste the social cost
is considerably less than suggested by these data. Thus, in 1965 about

now afford, sometimes reminding of goods that gave satisfaction before.[59]

Advertising plays a major role in our economy because new
products are offered in ever greater numbers, and existing
products must be called to the attention of new consumers who
are added to the market as a result of expansion in incomes,
the population explosion, and changes in tastes. Potential
markets also expand as incomes rise and as consumers are able
to purchase products they could not afford previously. Con-
tinuous large-scale advertising is necessary to provide re-
minders to old customers and to provide information to new
customers.

Often this information[60] is required to create interest in
and demand for a product.[61] Thus, it has been reported:

> ... to a significant degree General Foods and the U. S.
> food market created each other. Before a new product appears,
> customers are rarely conscious of wanting it. There was no
> spontaneous demand for ready-to-eat cereal; frozen foods
> required a sustained marketing effort stretching over many
> years; instant coffee had been around for decades, supply-

$9 billion was spent on advertising in newspapers, magazines, radio, and
television; another $700 million was spent on farm and business publi-
cations. Without these expenditures, these sources of news and entertainment would have had to obtain substantial sums from other sources.
It has been estimated that " . . . advertising paid for over 60 percent of
the cost of periodicals, for over 70 percent of the cost of newspapers, and
for 100 per cent of the cost of commercial radio and TV broadcasting."
Fritz Machlup, *The Production and Distribution of Knowledge in the United
States,* Princeton University Press, Princeton, New Jersey, 1962, p. 265.

59 John W. Hobson, "The Freedom of the Marketplace," An Address
Before the 57th Annual Meeting of the Association of National Advertisers,
Colorado Springs, Colorado, October 1966, p. 4.

60 It has been observed: "Advertising is selling ... The object of advertising is ... to inform for the purpose of selling." John Hobson, "The Influence
and Techniques of Modern Advertising," *Journal of the Royal Society of
Arts,* July 1964, p. 2.

61 Professor E. H. Chamberlin of Harvard University has observed:
"Certainly new products and new varieties of old products would have
virtually no market at all without selling outlays of this sort [advertising]."
E. H. Chamberlin, *The Theory of Monopolistic Competition,* Fifth Edition,
Harvard University Press, Cambridge, Mass., 1946, p. 119.

ing a market that did not amount to a tenth of its present
level. General Foods' corporate skill consists largely in know-
ing enough about American tastes to foresee what products
will be accepted.[62]

The critics of advertising are really attacking the competitive process. Competition involves considerable duplication
and "waste." The illustrations range from the several gaso-
line stations at an important intersection to the multiplication of research facilities, the excess industrial capacity
which develops during periods of expansion, and the accumu-
lations of excessive inventories.[63]

We cannot judge the efficiency of our competitive
society—including the various instrumentalities, such as
advertising—by looking at the negative aspects alone. It is
true that competition involves waste. But it also yields a
flood of new products, improved quality, better service,
and pressures on prices. In the United States, it has facilitated
enormous economic growth with the accompanying high
standards of living. The advantages of competition have been
so overwhelmingly greater than the wastes that we have established as one of our prime national goals the continuance
of a competitive economy.[64]

The charge of large-scale waste in advertising appears
to reflect in part a yearning for an economy with standardized,
homogeneous products which are primarily functional in
nature. An illustration would be a refrigerator which is de-

---

62 "General Foods Is Five Billion Particulars," *Fortune,* March 1964,
p. 117. Similarly, J. K. Galbraith has observed: "A new consumer product
must be introduced with a suitable advertising capaign to arouse an interest
in it. The path for an expansion of output must be paved by a suitable
expansion in the advertising budget. Outlays for the manufacturing of a
product are not more important in the strategy of modern business enterprise than outlays for the manufacturing of demand for the product."
J. K. Galbraith, *The Affluent Society,* Houghton Mifflin Company, Boston,
Mass., 1958, p. 156.

63 C. H. Sandage and Vernon Fryburger, *Advertising Theory and
Practice,* Sixth Edition, Richard D. Irwin, Inc., Homewood, Ill., 1963,
p. 38 and Borden, *op. cit.,* p. 486.

64 The antitrust laws illustrate our desire to achieve this objective.

signed solely to be technically efficient for the storage of food. However, customers are also interested in the decor of their kitchen, in convenience and speed in the manufacture of ice cubes, in shelves which rotate, thus increasing accessibility, and in special storage for butter. Similarly, a purchaser wants more than transportation from an automobile; he may also desire style, social status, comfort, and prestige. These are additions to functional usefulness which "an affluent society" can afford but which a subsistence economy cannot. In the latter situation, these "extras" may divert some resources from meeting the basic necessities of life, but this does not necessarily apply in a high-consumption economy like ours.

The entire concept of waste must be related to the level achieved by an economy. Professor John W. Lowe has observed that "Perhaps a good deal of the 'wastefulness' assigned to advertising springs from the fact that a large part of the world's population cannot consider satisfying psychological wants when most of their efforts must be devoted to *needs*."[65] (Italics added)

In a subsistence economy, scarcity is so significant that advertising might be wasteful, particularly where it diverts resources from meeting the basic necessities of life. In contrast, in the high-level American economy, there usually are surpluses rather than scarcity. The use of resources for advertising and to differentiate products does not represent a diversion from other uses. Rather, in most instances it represents the use of resources that might otherwise be idle[66] both in the the short run and the long run, and this use may obviate the waste that such idleness represents.

The concept of waste cannot ignore the question—waste as compared with what alternative? Advertising cannot be considered in a vacuum. It is one of the marketing alternatives

65 John W. Lowe, "An Economist Defends Advertising," *Journal of Marketing,* July 1963, p. 18. See also Harry G. Johnson, *The Canadian Quandary, Economic Problems and Policies,* McGraw-Hill Company of Canada, Limited, Toronto, 1963, pp. 279-81.

66 It must be recognized, of course, that some manpower might be shifted to alternative uses.

available. Generally it is not a question of advertising or nothing but rather of advertising or some other type of sales effort. In this connection, Richard Tennant has noted: "Advertising often turns out to be the most effective way of appealing to customers for a given expenditure or the least expensive in terms of resources used to secure a given appeal."[67]

We live in an economy that has little resemblance to the ideals of perfect competiton postulated by economists. In such an idealized economy, advertising would be wasteful, since it would have a very minor role to play. But in the world of reality, this is not true. Advertising is an integral and vital part of our growing economy and plays an important role in the launching of the new products so essential to economic growth.

Perfect Competition Yardstick

To evaluate the role of advertising, the economist's yardstick of pure or perfect competition is not an appropriate measure.[68] In the idealized world of perfect competition there would be little need for most advertising because products would be identical and hence completely substitutable.[69] But in the real world these conditions are rarely found.

The prerequisites for pure or perfect competition include: 1] such a large number of buyers and sellers that no one can influence the price; 2] the production of homogeneous or standardized products; 3] freedom of entry into

67 Richard B. Tennant, "Advertising, Competition and the Antitrust Laws," 26 *ABA Antitrust section* (August 10-13, 1964), p. 173. See also Sandage and Fryburger, *op. cit.,* p. 57. Otto Kleppner has made this same point most succinctly in his observation that: "A reason so many manufacturers of consumer products use advertising is that they have found *advertising is the way to tell many people about a product in the fastest time at the lowest cost per message.*"Kleppner, *op. cit.,* p. 546.

68 The terms *pure competition* and *perfect competition* often are used interchangeably, although there are some technical distinctions between them. Imperfect competition describes an economy in which the conditions assumed for pure or perfect competition are not present—that is, the real world.

69 " . . . the wastes of competitive advertising are characteristic

and exit from an industry, that is, free mobility of resources; 4] an economy operating at full capacity; 5] a static economy, that is, one in which incomes, tastes, and habits remain unchanged; 6] full knowledge by buyers of all the alternatives available.

This is the theoretical ideal of competition. However, it does not exist in the real world except to some extent on the commodity and stock exchanges. For some products, one or more of the foregoing prerequisites may prevail, but in general they are not found in the combination indicated in any part of our economy except possibly agriculture.

The number of sellers usually is considerably smaller than postulated because some industries would be completely inefficient if each producer were small enough to meet this test, (e.g., autos, steel, aluminum). Thus, the possibility of economies of scale in a dynamic economy means that the achievement of the objective of pure or perfect competition would not be feasible. Some raw materials are standardized (e.g., wheat, cotton, copper), but manufactured goods generally are not (most chemicals and steel provide exceptions when they are produced to designated specifications). Product differentiation rather than standardization characterizes practically all consumer goods. Ease of entry into some markets is difficult for many reasons, including heavy capital requirements, patents, or lack of distribution systems.[70]

We have a dynamic economy. Tastes change and incomes expand with different groups sharing unevenly. Some products increase in favor at the expense of others (margarine in place of butter). New products and modifications of old ones proliferate and increase the alternatives available

---

of monopolistic, not a perfect, competition. In perfect competition . . . there is no advertising of a competitive nature," Boulding, *op. cit.,* p. 514.

70 J.M. Clark has pointed out: "To bring about 'perfect' competition, free and costless exit as well as free entry is necessary and the fact that it is impossible is the chief reason why 'perfect competition' must always remain imaginary." *Op. cit.,* p. 112.

to consumers (e.g., instant coffee, detergents, transistor radios, spray-on deodorants). The large number of products available makes it impossible for the consumer to have much knowledge about many, although he or she quickly determines whether a product lives up to advance claims.

Thus, when the economist sets up perfect competition as a yardstick for measurement it must be recognized that it is not attainable. Clair Wilcox has pointed out: "The concept is useful merely as a standard by which to measure the varying degrees of imperfection that must always characterize the actual markets in which goods are bought and sold. It cannot be taken as a practical objective of public policy."[71] What the economist really is saying is that we should move in the direction of this ideal, not that we can, will, or should attain it. But the distance between the ideal and reality is so great that it usually is unrealistic to use the ideal as a yardstick.

Summary and Conclusions

The marked expansion in our national economy during the past quarter of a century has been accompanied by a sevenfold rise in total advertising expenditures. Such expenditures have more than kept pace with national economic growth so that advertising has been a larger proportion of personal consumption expenditures since the mid-1950's than in the pre-World War II period.

After adjusting for price changes, advertising expenditures in real terms more than tripled in the postwar period as compared with the doubling of real personal consumption expenditures. It seems far more probable that the rise in economic activity has caused the rise in advertising than the reverse.

The rise in relative importance of advertising reflects several developments including: the new product explosion,

71 *Public Policies Toward Business,* Third Edition, Richard D. Irwin, Inc., Homewood, Ill., 1966, p. 252.

the development of television as a major new advertising medium, the sharp rise in discretionary incomes, and the increasing intensity of competition. The phenomenal expansion of industrial research and development has led to vast improvements in older products and to an increasing array of new ones. A relatively high advertising cost often is required to launch new and improved products. The simultaneous increase in discretionary incomes has meant a marked expansion in the market for such products.

There is no way to determine a cutoff point above which "advertising is too high" either in dollars or as a per cent of sales volume. The situation in each company and industry must be evaluated separately. The relative importance of new products, the role played by other marketing tools, the nature of the product (consumer's good v. industrial product), competitive pressures—these and other factors determine the meaningfulness of any level of advertising expenditures.

Without high advertising expenditures, the new products which contribute so significantly to the well-being of consumers and to national economic growth would not develop mass markets, and in the absence of the possibility of such markets, there would be little incentive for large-scale research and development. Thus, national economic activity and advertising act and interact to induce higher levels for both.

Advertising does not take place in a vacuum. It is one of several marketing alternatives which may be selected at the option of a company, although competitive pressures may result in greater emphasis upon one or more of these alternatives. The abandonment of advertising could not represent a net saving to a company or to the economy. Instead, such a development would require a shift to alternative marketing techniques, some of which undoubtedly would be less efficient than advertising, since companies do not deliberately adopt the least effective marketing approach. Such a shift would indeed be wasteful.

There is wide agreement that advertising provides very

useful information which plays a significant role in our highly complex economy. Although precise data are not available, it appears that the charge that advertising represents economic waste refers to substantially less than half of all advertising expenditures. Most types of competition involve duplication and waste. Competition in advertising is no exception. But if the accent is placed solely on the negative, a distorted picture is obtained. On balance, the contribution of competition to our economy has more than overbalanced the wastes, and the same is true for competition in advertising. The charge of large-scale waste in advertising appears to reflect in part a yearning for an economy with standardized, homogeneous products which are primarily functional in nature.

The effectiveness of advertising depends upon the characteristics of an industry's products. Many more advertising dollars are spent on consumer goods than for industrial products. The proportions spent for advertising vary widely among consumer goods and even for the same product as companies adopt different marketing strategies. It is most widely used for relatively low-priced brand-name items available from many retail establishments and subject to frequent repeat purchases. These are brutally competitive markets in which new products and new brands become available frequently.

Total consumer disposable income rather than advertising is the major determinant of aggregate consumer demand. However, advertising may affect total demand through its contribution to the launching of new products. Advertising together with other factors (for example, relative prices, packaging, changes in composition of the population, distribution facilities, tastes, religion, geography, and customs) helps to influence the extent to which companies and industries will receive some share of the consumer's dollar.

Despite the many criticisms of large-scale advertising, there is only a small number of products for which there is a high intensity of advertising. An estimated 5% to 6% of the expenditures of a moderate-income family is for products—

largely new ones—for which advertising accounts for 5% or more of manufacturers' sales.

Although advertising would have little role in the economist's idealized world of pure or perfect competition, it is of great significance in our dynamic, if imperfectly competitive, economy. Therefore, it is unrealistic to use the norms of perfect competition to test the economic desirability of advertising.

III

Advertising and Barriers to Entry

Ease of entry into a market long has been regarded as one of the key indicia of a competitive market structure. The courts have given this factor considerable emphasis in judging the legality of mergers.[1] Heavy advertising expenditures have been viewed by some critics as creating barriers to entry[2] because present producers develop such goodwill for their products that newcomers must spend large sums on advertising to compete effectively.[3] Thus, it allegedly limits entry in two ways: 1] The volume of resources required to compete is very great; this limits the entry of small firms into the market, and 2] it is difficult to overcome existing brand loyalties; this acts as a deterrent to larger firms.[4]

1 Betty Bock, *Mergers and Markets,* 3rd edition, National Industrial Conference Board, New York, 1964, pp. 38-39, 188-96.

2 McConnell, *op. cit.,* p. 513.

3 " . . . the larger the size of, and the greater the amount of 'goodwill attached to the representative firm' in any particular trade, the larger is the initial outlay which must be risked by a potential newcomer who wishes to invade the market." Kaldor, *op. cit.,* p. 15. See also The Monopolies Commission, *Household Detergents,* Her Majesty's Stationery Office, London, England, August 3, 1966, p. 37.

4 The Supreme Court stated in the American Tobacco case that

FTC Economist Willard Mueller has observed "It seems probable that advertising-created and maintained product differentiation constitutes the *chief barrier* confronting prospective entrants in many grocery product industries."[5] (Italics added.) Similarly, it has been claimed that the advertising-rate structure for television tends "to limit the entry of new competitors" into consumer-goods industries.

The basic criticism has been summarized by Assistant Attorney General Donald F. Turner as follows:[6]

> To an extent, the increased barrier to entry created by advertising is a price we have to pay for providing consumers with information. But *when heavy advertising and other promotional expenditures create durable preferences going beyond the relative superiority of the product, resistant to anything but major countervailing promotional campaigns,* we may well question whether the price has not become too high. If heavy advertising expenditures thus serve to raise the barriers to entry, the adverse competitive consequences are important not only because new firms are kept out, but also because frequently it is the *prospect of new entry which*

"Such tremendous advertising . . . is also a widely published warning that these companies possess and know how to use a powerful offensive and defensive weapon against new competition." *American Tobacco Co. v. United States,* 328 U S 797 (1946). The U. S. Court of Appeals stated, however, that price differentials made advertising impotent. See Gilbert H. Weil, "Advertising, Competition, and the Antitrust Laws: The Challenge to Traditional Legal Concepts," *26 ABA Antitrust Section,* p. 201.

5 Willard Mueller, "Processor vs. Distributor Brands in Food Distribution," An Address Before the National Council of Farm Cooperatives, Houston, Texas, January 13, 1964, p. 5. However, Dr. Mueller also pointed out that "distributor-brand" products have played a major role in food chain stores. "Whereas 62 percent of the 10 largest chains' purchases were under their own brands, 28 percent of the purchases of all other chains were under their own brands, and less than 18 percent of nonchain retailers' purchases were under their own brands." *Ibid.,* p. 8. See also *The Structure of Food Manufacturing,* Technical Study No. 8, National Commission on Food Marketing, Washington, D. C., June 1966, p. 200. These private brands also may be a barrier to entry into the chain-store market.

6 Harlan M. Blake and Jack A. Blum, "Network Television Rate-

> *serves as a major competitive restraint* upon the actions of existing firms . . .
>
> . . . *entry will be made more difficult as a result of the barriers created through extensive advertising.* To the extent that consumers are unable to evaluate the relative merits of competing products, the established products may have a considerable advantage and it is this advantage that advertising messages tend to accentuate. High entry barriers interfere with the normal process through which increases in demand are met at least in part by *new firms.*[7] [Italics added]

All observers do not agree with these charges. Thus, Professor Lester G. Telser of the University of Chicago has observed: "Increased advertising, far from signifying an obstacle to entry, is very often symptomatic of the reverse. It is the high turnover of brands and sometimes of firms that accounts for the large advertising outlays on some products . . . Advertising is frequently a means of entry and a sign of competition."[8]

Power of the Purse

That large companies have greater financial resources available for all purposes than smaller companies is not exactly an earth-shaking conclusion. They also usually have more extensive research and development, economies of scale, more extensive distribution systems, more experienced management, etc. On the other hand, there are also dis-

---

Practices: A Case Study in the Failure of Social Control of Price Discrimination," *Yale Law Journal,* July 1965, pp. 1375-76. In 1966, the three television networks revised their rate schedules to eliminate all discounts except a "modest continuity discount" for consecutive use of TV time in a 52 week period. (Testimony of major television executives before the Senate Subcommittee on Antitrust and Monopoly (Hart Committee), December 13 and 14, 1966.) This testimony also presented data which show the similarity of costs to large and small advertisers and the availability of prime time to both.

7 Turner, *op. cit.,* pp. 2-3. See also "Reith Report," *op. cit.,* p. 38.

8 Lester G. Telser, "Advertising and Competition," *Journal of Political Economy,* December 1964, pp. 556, 558. See also Alderson, *op. cit.,* p. 122.

advantages to size, including inflexibility and bureaucracy. It is the composite of these factors which characterizes large companies.

The "large purse" theory assumes that competition can only take place on a national scale and hence requires large expenditures for advertising. But in many areas, local companies compete successfully with national companies.[9] They can advertise extensively within a limited budget by using local newspapers, spot radio, spot television, and more recently, regional editions of national magazines.

A study for the National Commission of Food Marketing concluded that for dry groceries, despite the barriers to entry into national markets because of nonprice competition and "rising capital requirements," " . . . the small manufacturer, competing regionally or locally with an innovative product, still should be able to market successfully."[10] Moreover, small companies often compete by developing substitute products. A Federal Trade Commission study of the food industry noted that "The initial producers of most of these new [food] products were characteristically smaller firms."[11] Thus, there are many smaller companies which thrive and in time become large companies. Regional and local companies compete successfully with national companies.

The 20 largest food manufacturing companies accounted for 71% of the food advertising on network television and 60% of the total in magazines in 1964. Since advertising in magazines does not present quite the same high financial cost as that on television, the close relationship between the shares in both media is of interest. Moreover, the FTC study reported that these 20 largest companies "were somewhat less important in the regional media such as spot television

9 Peckham, "Formula For Marketing New Brands of Toilet Goods," *op. cit.,* pp. 9-10. See also Jack B. Weiner, "Myth of the National Market," *Dun's Review and Modern Industry,* May 1964, pp. 41-43, 107-108, 110.

10 "Grocery Manufacturing," *op. cit.,* pp. 50-51.

11 "The Structure of Food Manufacturing," *op. cit.,* p. 81.

and newspapers, where they accounted for about 38 percent of all food advertising in these media."[12] Apparently, the "size of the purse" was a less important barrier regionally. Smaller companies can afford to meet the lower costs of advertising on a local or regional basis and in some instances may play a key role in such areas.

Lesser-known or private brands also can and do provide effective competition to many national brands in many parts of the country. Private brands are particularly important for food products and, as is noted later, often have a larger share of a market than the national brands with which they compete. Thus, large advertising expenditures will not necessarily improve the position of the big firm in the market.

Nicholas H. Kaldor has contended "... the 'pulling power' of the larger [advertising] expenditure must overshadow that of smaller ones with the consequence that the larger firms are bound to gain at the expense of the smaller ones."[13] This assumption that large companies will continually increase their share of the market because of their financial resources is not supported by experience. It would be difficult to convince many companies of the validity of this thesis. Included among the doubters would be Coca-Cola, Schlitz, American Tobacco, U. S. Steel, Alcoa, and many others which have seen their relative market shares decline sharply or which have lost their number one position. Actually, there

12 "The Structure of Food Manufacturing," *op. cit.,* p. 66.

13 Kaldor, *op. cit.,* p. 13. In the Procter & Gamble-Clorox case, the Federal Trade Commission emphasized the role of massive advertising and promotion. It charged that " . . . Procter could obtain larger discounts than Clorox in television network, newspaper and magazine advertising, and could adapt the advertising on a national or local basis as the need arises." However, the U. S. Circuit Court of Appeals concluded: "We cannot assume that Procter would divert the large sums which it found necessary to expend for advertising and promotion to maintain its competitive position in the soap cleanser field to wipe out its competitors in the household bleach market." (U. S. Circuit Court of Appeals for the Sixth Circuit, Decided March 18, 1966. This decision set aside the FTC order with instructions to dismiss complaint. Commerce Clearing House, *Trade Regulation Reporter,* Vol. 5, pp. 82, 182-83.) In October 1966, the United States Supreme Court agreed to review this decision.

is quite a gap between the availability of large financial resources and an increase or even stability in market shares,
as will be noted later.

The ability to spend money is only part of the advertising story. Henry M. Schachte has pointed out:

> All advertising consists essentially of just three parts—
> first, the basic idea . . . second, the skill with which this idea
> is presented to the market place; and third our plan for put-
> ting our messages before the people . . . [a] study showed
> that in an analysis of over 50 million dollars' worth of tele-
> vision advertising, *the effectiveness of the advertising mess-
> age, in communicating a meaningful and important promise,
> was some three times as effective as changes in the level
> of advertising expenditure in actually influencing sales results.*
>
>   . . . Large advertising expenditures don't guarantee mar-
> keting success. Larger expenditures don't guarantee more
> volume on behalf of one product than do smaller investments
> on behalf of another one.[14] (Italics added.)

Similarly, Richard B. Tennant has observed that: ". . .
the quality of advertising may be just as important as the
breadth and intensity of its coverage . . . There are dimin-
ishing returns to advertising as there are to all uses of resources."[15]

Fundamentally, a company must have a good product
and one which is acceptable to the consumer[16] not only func-

14 Henry M. Schachte, "Advertising, Competition and the Antitrust Laws: The View From the Market Place," *26 ABA Antitrust Section,*
pp. 163-65. Harold M. Spielman of the Schwerin Research Corporation
conducted a study of 53 national television campaigns and concluded that:
" . . . the weight of money behind the advertising did not, in and of itself,
produce more sales." "Characteristics of the Aggressive Advertiser," An
Address Before The British Columbia Chapter of American Marketing
Association, March 18, 1964, pp. 2 and 4. See also Robert D. Buzzell,
"Predicting Short-Term Changes in Market Share as a Function of Advertising Strategy," *Journal of Marketing Research,* August 1964, pp. 30-31.

15 Tennant, *op. cit.,* p. 175.

16 For illustrations of products which were not successful although
heavily advertised by such companies as General Mills, General Foods,
American Tobacco, Bristol-Myers, and others, see Burt Schorr, "Many
Products Fizzle Despite Careful Planning, Publicity," in *Contemporary*

tionally but in terms of many intangible factors such as prestige, aesthetics, and relative quality. The failure to meet these objectives also can be a significant barrier to entry. This is particularly true for products which are subject to frequent repeat purchases at relatively low prices because the consumer has ample repetitive opportunity to compare performance against claims. Large-scale advertising expenditure for an inferior product is foredoomed to failure.

That there are products for which entry is difficult because of financial reasons is undoubtedly true. But there are so many exceptions to this generalization that it must be used with care. Each situation where entry may be difficult must be separately analyzed to determine whether the barrier is the cost of advertising or some other factor.[17]

Bain Study

Professor Joe S. Bain often is cited in support of the thesis that product differentiation combined with heavy advertising provide powerful barriers to entry.[18] After studying 20 industries, Bain concluded that 6 were characterized by "great product-differentiation barriers." In this latter group, there were only 3 "for which apparent actual advertising costs are high"—cigarettes,[19] liquor, and quality fountain pens.[20] The other three industries with great product differentiation but relatively modest advertising costs were auto-

---

American Marketing, edited by Harper W. Boyd, Jr. and Richard M. Clewett, Revised Edition, Richard D. Irwin, Homewood, Ill., 1962, pp. 113-18.

17 Mark Massel has concluded: "There are no overt guides for gauging ease of entry into a market. Therefore, analysis of this factor depends on several subsidiary issues: patents, trade barriers, costs, discounts, product differentiation, and previous history of entries and exits." Massel, *op. cit.,* p. 199.

18 Joe S. Bain, *Barriers To New Competition,* Harvard University Press, Cambridge, Mass., 1956. The author concluded: " . . . the most important barrier to entry . . . is probably product differentiation." (p. 216)

19 Between 1956, when Bain's volume was published, and 1966, the change in relative importance of brands was particularly dramatic.

20 With the development of the inexpensive ball point pen in recent years, this is hardly a good illustration currently.

mobiles, tractors and farm machinery, and typewriters. He also stated that "the advantages of very-large scale advertising are possibly present" for soap, consumer-brand flour, and canned soups and other specialty canned products.[21] However, these industries were classified by Bain as "having moderate product-differentiation barriers of entry on the average."[22] These data provide little support for Bain's thesis.[23]

In addition, Bain clearly stated that the available data were not very satisfactory. Thus, he noted that the hypothesis that:

> There should generally tend to be a positive association between the height of the product-differentiation barrier to the entry to an industry and the size (measured probably as a percentage of sales) of its costs of sales promotion . . . rest on the suppositions (1) that stronger product differentiation is ordinarily accompanied by or rests upon larger selling costs: and (2) that higher product-differentiation barriers to entry are generally erected and maintained by higher selling costs. Testing of this hypothesis is made difficult by the *inadequacy of available data.*[24] (*Italics added.*)

To test this hypothesis, Professor Bain used FTC data for 1944 and some additional information for 1950. However, he warned that these data

> . . . do not lend themselves well to analyses involving inter-industry comparisons of advertising costs . . . The difficulty with these data is that it is *impossible to determine* what proportion of the designated costs are properly classifiable as "sales promotional" and what proportion ascribable to routine distribution. In consequence, *only the roughest sort of judgments* can be made concerning the relation of actual sales promotion costs to the height of the product-differentiation barrier to entry.[25] (*Italics added.*)

21 *Ibid.,* p. 137.   22 *Ibid.,* p. 202.

23 Despite advertising costs which "seem astonishingly high," Bain classified soap as a product with "moderate product-differentiation barriers to entry, but it is evidently on the borderline between the 'moderate' and 'great' barriers categories, and could readily be put in the latter." *Ibid.,* pp. 281-85.

24 *Ibid.,* pp. 201-2.   25 *Ibid.,* p. 202.

In light of these qualifications, Bain concluded: "These tentative findings are not inconsistent with our hypothesis, but they could scarcely be said to verify it in detail."[26] Despite this relatively weak conclusion, many writers cite the Bain study as though it provided definitive proof that advertising creates an important barrier to entry.

Some Key Questions

In evaluating the significance of "barriers to entry" several questions must be kept in mind. How is the market to be defined? What is meant by entry — the entry of newly organized firms or of existing large and small firms, not now in the market, who may diversify by producing the product involved? Is it recognized that existing smaller firms already in the industry may provide successful competition and possibly move ahead of the present leaders? Or that imports may provide substantial competition, as for radios, cameras, low priced cars, and other products? How much consideration is given to the number of products already available and to the intensity of competition among them? Doesn't the turnover of products and firms in the market over time reflect dynamic competition and suggest that product differentiation is not always accompanied by a degree of brand loyalty which enables a company to exploit an alleged "monopoly" position?

HOW IS THE MARKET DEFINED?

Whether firms can enter the product market depends in part upon how that market is defined. The narrowest definition would confine the market only to the most heavily advertised national brands while the broadest definition would include products which are readily substitutable; between these extremes the market would consist only of the products which are similar to the well-known brands. The differences in these market concepts can be illustrated by aspirin. The narrowest definition would confine the market

26 *Ibid.*, p. 203.

to the few well-advertised brands of aspirin. The broadest definition would extend the market to all headache remedies. The intermediate definition would define the market as all aspirin—heavily advertised, lightly advertised, and private brands.

Markets which include heavily advertised brands, many lesser-known brands and private brands often carve out a niche by establishing a price differential as compared with the well-known brands. For these companies advertising cannot be considered a barrier to entry.

WHO ARE THE NEW ENTRANTS?

Reference frequently is made to the barriers of entry to "new" firms,[27] or to "new entrants."[28] The latter term is much broader, since it embraces entry by existing firms as well as by new firms. Accordingly, it is more meaningful to consider the problem on that basis. New entrants may be divided into three categories: 1] existing large firms whether or not they are already in the industry; 2] local and regional firms already in the product market; 3] new firms. Competitive pressures may develop from any or all of these categories. Some critics seem to believe that only if new firms are created to enter a market will there be a competitive impact. Such a view is highly unrealistic, since the most effective competition may develop from other large companies, not previously in that product market.

The most likely new competitor in a given product market is another large company which is already in the industry and desires to lengthen its product line. Every company in an industry does not always produce a full line of products. As profitable opportunities appear, new lines are added. A good illustration is the entry into the cold-tablet market by Menley & James, a subsidiary of Smith, Kline, and French (Contac).[29]

27 Turner, *op. cit.,* p. 3.
28 Bain, "Industrial Organization," *op. cit.,* pp. 174-75.
29 For a discussion of the success of this product see *Advertising Age,* November 28, 1966, pp. 3, 100.

In recent years, the conglomerate company—one that produces unrelated goods in a number of industries—has become increasingly important in the American economy. There is a far greater possibility than in the past of new entry into a market by large companies from other industries whenever profits are attractive (e.g. Armour, a meat packer, entering the soap market with Dial). The need to invest large sums in advertising need not be a barrier to such companies.[30] Lack of know-how about the product, the inability to develop a family of products, need for new channels of distribution —these and other factors can be more important barriers to success than lack of availability of advertising dollars (e.g. Monsanto's experience with All). But when such companies enter a market they can be powerful competitors.

Another important potential group of new entrants into markets with nationally advertised products are smaller companies already in the industry. These concerns may have expanded from local to regional markets before taking the plunge at the national level. They have experience with the product and have had an opportunity to build up a reputation for quality. By extending their markets from one region to another they can become strong competitive factors in those areas and in time on a national basis.[31]

30 However, the British Monopolies Commission attributed the failure of "some of the more obvious potential competitors, such as large chemical manufacturers" to enter the detergent market to their reluctance "to participate in - and by participating perhaps to intensify—the process of competition in promotion expenditure which appears to prevail in the industry." "Household Detergents, *op. cit.,* p. 36.

31 Brink and Kelley have reported " . . . a small business man may become large if he comes up with a superior product and knows how to advertise and sell it effectively. A small, but well-used, sales and advertising budget has launched many a product on the road to success. For example, the initial expenditure on advertising for Glass Wax was $50,000; for Toni, $5,000; and for Jules Montenier (Stopette), $55,000 for all promotion," Edward L. Brink and William T. Kelley, *The Management of Promotion,* Prentice-Hall, Englewood Cliffs, N. J., 1963, p. 300. An interesting case study of how a small Canadian company, Household Cleaners Ltd., expanded its sales of blue Jets soap pads from a local to a national basis is described by J.R. Grainger in *How To Introduce A New Product Against An Established Brand,* An Address before the Association of

The third group consists of newly organized companies. These are the companies most likely to be deterred from starting on a national scale not only because of the requirement for a heavy investment in advertising but more importantly because of the need to build up manufacturing know-how and capacity with the accompanying large capital required and the difficulty of "going national" without a family of products. Actually few new manufacturing companies can now start on a national basis. Years of experience are required before a company can operate on the national level with some chance of success. New companies usually begin by obtaining a toehold in an industry on a smaller scale, either locally or regionally. Initially, they may establish a price differential to overcome at least in part the reluctance of consumers to buy unfamiliar products or from untested sources.

The availability of potential competition also acts as a restraint against existing producers. The number of potential competitors is less important than their size and their availability.[32] Thus, the fact that financial barriers do not keep out other large companies is the most important aspect of entry in terms of its competitive effect.

The competition faced by a major national brand is from a composite of all of the types of firms noted above. There are some nationally known brands with which it must compete across the country, there are other brands with which it must compete in smaller geographic areas,[33] and there are unbranded products which feature lower prices with which it also competes on a local basis. The lineup of competitors, therefore, may vary among markets. It is the fact of competition in each of these markets which is important, not the specific national reputation of the brands with which it must compete.[34]

Canadian Advertisers, Inc., in Toronto, Canada, May 2-4, 1966.

32 Jules Backman, "Joint Ventures and the Antitrust Laws," *New York University Law Review,* October 1965, pp. 668-71.

33 There will be varying local or regional brands in different parts of the country.

34 National brands achieve varying degrees of market penetration

Dynamic Competition and Market Shares

The establishment of brand names has become a key element in the marketing of consumer goods. A brand distinguishes a product from competitive products and is an integral part of product differentiation. This development has led to the charge that companies obtain excessive market power through the use of brands.

Does product differentiation, through the establishment of brands, make it possible for a company to insulate itself against competitive pressures and hence to establish some degree of monopoly? By building brand loyalty can a company pre-empt part of a market to itself even if its product is higher in price than a competitive one? Some critics of advertising answer these questions in the affirmative.

Practically every market situation is an amalgam of elements of monopoly and of competition. As an example, every retail store has a monopoly related to the site on which it is located. Some locations are much more advantageous than others usually because of traffic patterns. In these terms, a "Mom and Pop" store has elements of monopoly. Nevertheless, no one is concerned about the social consequences of this "monopoly" because of the competitive — and usually powerfully competitive — alternatives available to consumers.

Similarly, a brand gives a product an identification which differentiates it from those of its competitors. The company that owns the brand has a "monopoly" of its use. This is the reason why economists talk about the market power which accompanies product differentiation. Never-

---

in different sections of the country. Thus, a 1966 Pulse, Inc. study of eight cities showed that Budweiser beer ranked first in Boston with 22.5% of the market but eighth in Philadelphia with only 2.2% and fifth in Baltimore with 5.3%. Among hairsprays, Alberto VO-5 was first in Boston with 12.4%, second in San Francisco with 8.4%, and third in Pittsburgh with 13.2%. Reproduced in *Advertising Age,* November 21, 1966, p. 136. For similar data for 20 product categories in seven marketing areas prepared by Audits and Surveys, see *Advertising Age,* January 30, 1967, p. 124.

theless, the existence of the brand is not the totality of the market situation. Usually, the brand must compete with a wide variety of other products including other national brands, private labels, unbranded products sold at a lower price, and substitute products.

The basic question is which of these two broad forces is more powerful: the monopoly of the brand or the competitive pressures exerted by the other products available? The answer is found in the history of market shares. If the brand is the dominant factor, then the product should be able to maintain or even increase its share of the market over time. Moreover, the pattern of market shares accounted for by different brands should not change markedly over time. Presumably each one carves its niche and in the absence of a major change in the nature of the product or a breakthrough in promotional techniques would retain a relatively static share of the market.[35]

On the other hand, if competitive pressures overcome and hence outweigh the "market power" of a brand, market shares should change.[36] And the more overpowering the competitive pressures, the more dramatic the changes in market shares. The possession of market power does not mean control of a market; they are neither identical nor interchangeable concepts.

Actual experience indicates that the "market power" associated with brands usually is not very potent. Even where brand loyalty is developed, it does not determine the buying habits of all purchasers. Varying proportions of the purchasers of all categories of products have weak brand loyalties.[37]

35 It must be recognized, of course, that market shares may remain relatively unchanged even for products for which advertising is not very intensive.

36 For an excellent discussion of the distinctions between market share and market power, see Joel Dean and Warren Gustus, "Vertical Integration and Section 7," *New York University Law Review,* October 1965, pp. 688-91.

37 "... in our dynamic economy between 20% and 40% of the regular

A survey at the supermarket checkout counter showed that customers had switched brands for the following reasons:

Special display and/or store feature	25%
Cheaper	21
Just wanted a change	19
Recommended	9
Usual brand out-of-stock	7
Stamps, sample or coupon	6
Saw or heard it advertised	4
Other	9
TOTAL	100

The study concluded that supermarket shoppers are " . . . shifting brands continually and to such an extent that brand switching has become one of the national advertiser's major headaches." [38]

Ross Cunningham studied the buying habits of 50 Chicago families for 18 categories of food products in 1956.[39] He found that single brand loyalty ranged from an average of 83.5% for all-purpose flour and 82.8% for tea down to 54.6% for canned peaches and 55.7% for frozen juices. For the 18 product categories, there were 757 instances of single-brand loyalty. However, 217 instances represented loyalty to private brands.

The shifts of consumer purchasing habits in response to price differentials, to more effective advertising, to dis-

purchasers of a brand (those who say it is the brand they buy most often) will switch away from that brand within a 6-month period." Norton Garfinkle, *The Marketing Value of Media Audiences—How to Pinpoint Your Prime Prospects,* An Address before the A.N.A. Workshop on Advertising Planning and Evaluation, Plaza Hotel, New York, January 19, 1965, p. 13.

38 *Progressive Grocer,* April 1965, p. 105.

39 White bread, regular coffee, instant coffee, tea, all-purpose flour, butter, margarine, vegetable shortening, salad dressing, canned spaghetti, canned peaches, canned pineapple, canned fruit cocktail, frozen juices, canned peas, canned corn, frozen vegetables, and canned tuna and bonita. Ross M. Cunningham, "Customer Loyalty To Store and Brand," *Harvard Business Review,* November-December, 1961, pp. 134-35. For his study of brand loyalty for toilet soap, scouring cleanser, frozen orange juice, and headache tablets see "Brand Loyalty—What, Where, How Much?" *Harvard Business Review,* January-February 1956, pp. 116-28.

satisfaction with a product, to health fads and scares, to desire to experiment with something new, and to other factors has tended to weaken or to overcome the market power of most brands. In fact, one experienced practitioner observed in 1964: "In almost no major consumer goods category, where advertising works its hardest, is there a brand on top today which held that position ten years ago."[40] Although this is a very strong statement, which is subject to some exceptions, there have been enormous shifts in the position of brands, as is outlined at a later point. As Neil Borden has noted: "The life cycles of brands have become shorter than they were in less dynamic times."[41]

Companies recognize their inability to develop complete brand loyalty when they offer a diversity of brands for similar products in order to appeal to different groups and to attract the patronage of those who are constantly experimenting or who are dissatisfied with other brands. The significant changes in the shares accounted for by brands in many product markets is a familiar phenomenon.

NEW BRANDS AND MARKET SHARES

The fact that existing brands do not develop sufficient brand loyalty to prevent erosion of market shares is indicated by the successful introduction of many new brands. Thus, for grocery products it has been reported:

> A survey by Progressive Grocer revealed that the average food manufacturer offered 73 different items in 1959. From 1959 to 1965, he successfully added 45 items—an increase of about 10 percent a year. Brands introduced after 1949 accounted for 35 percent of breakfast food sales in 1960, 66 percent of dry dog food, and 46 percent of margarine.[42]

40 Schachte, *op. cit.,* p. 161.
41 Borden, "The Role of Advertising in the Various Stages of Corporate and Economic Growth," *op. cit.,* p. 489.
42 "Grocery Manufacturing," *op. cit.,* p. 27. New products introduced after 1954 accounted for 23.3% of the sales of all cereals in 1964. *Ibid.,* p. 193. A. C. Nielsen has reported that the number of cold cereal brands available to the average shopper in chain stores increased from 38 in 1956

Robert S. Headen and James W. McKie concluded that for cereals "... while the average buyer at any given point in time is likely to have an acceptable and most preferred set of brands which she buys, the brands comprising this acceptable set are quite likely to change over time as new brands are made available."[43]

Similarly, an A. C. Nielsen study showed that "Back in 1950 ... the major advertised brands of dentifrice, deodorants, shave cream, and hair tonics averaged about 70% of the market. Today [1964] these same brands have only about 30% of the business. The difference between these two figures—40% of today's market—represents new brands that were not available in 1950."[44] These data reflect the significant changes in market shares referred to earlier.

New brands may be made available by a company whose brand is losing position or is being replaced. For some products, the company name is associated with the brand, and hence a shift from one brand to another may not be too meaningful. However, in many instances the consumer does not associate a company name with a brand. In such cases, it is clear that the monopolistic aspects attributed to product differentiation are relatively insignificant. In other words, a shift among brands of a company indicates a weakness in brand loyalty.

It sometimes seems to be assumed that advertisers can sell any product to the public. However, there are many illustrations to show that large-scale advertising by a well-known firm does not assure that a new product can be launched successfully[45] or that existing products will hold their market

---

to 56 in 1964; in independent stores the number increased from 25 to 41 brands. (Cited in *Ibid.,* p. 192.)

43 Robert S. Headen and James W. McKie, *The Structure, Conduct, and Performance of the Breakfast Cereal Industry: 1954-1964,* Arthur D. Little, Inc., Cambridge, Mass., 1966, pp. 37-38 cited in "Grocery Manufacturing", *op. cit.,* p. 195.

44 Peckham "Formula For Marketing New Brands of Toilet Goods," *op. cit.,* p. 1.

45 For a description of General Foods' lack of success with frozen

shares.   Perhaps the outstanding demonstration of this point in recent years was the failure of Ford to secure public acceptance of the Edsel as against the public's acceptance of the Mustang. The public must desire a product and be convinced of its superior quality before it will make large-scale purchases.

The multiplication of brands has been criticized because " . . . much product differentiation consists of minor variations in ingredients, shape, color, or the like."[46] But what is the alternative in a competitive economy? Shall we allocate special sectors of the market to different companies as is done under cartels? Or shall we prohibit the introduction of new brands which are not "genuinely new products," however that term is to be defined? Clearly, there are inefficiencies inherent in the competitive process. These must be incurred if the benefits of competition are to be realized. Competition is not without its costs as well as its benefits, but its net efficiency cannot be denied.

PRIVATE BRANDS

Private brands, which are relatively easy to establish, provide vigorous competition for many national brands, particularly foods. Chain stores often feature their own brands as they seek to establish a distinctive image and to build up customer loyalty. A study of sales of white bread, frozen orange-juice concentrate, and margarine by six corporate food chains, which accounted for about 7% of total food store sales in 1964, showed that private brands outsold manufacturer's brands in each of the years 1960 to 1963.[47]

---

baby foods and gourmet foods see "General Foods Is Five Billion Particulars," *Fortune,* March 1964, p. 163.

46 *Food From Farmer to Consumer,* Report of the National Commission on Food Marketing, June 1966, Washington D. C., p. 91. Professor Peter O. Steiner has concluded that " . . . rapid brand obsolescence (in toiletries, etc.) is a response to the needs of advertising, and not the other way round." *American Economic Review, Papers and Proceedings,* May 1966, p. 474.

47 Ray A. Goldberg, *The Dynamics of Brand Competition,* An Address Before the Mid-Year Meeting, Grocery Manufacturers of America,

The National Commission on Food Marketing made an extensive questionnaire survey of nine categories of food products to determine the relative importance of private labels.[48] The results are shown in Table III-1.

Table III-1
Private Labels as Percent of Sales for Retail Stores, Voluntary Group Wholesalers, and Cooperative Group Wholesalers, 1964-1965

	113 Retail Respondents	121 Voluntary Group Wholesalers	45 Cooperative Group Wholesalers (percent)
Canned vegetables	26.2	24.2	18.7
Canned fruit	30.1	23.1	23.8
Frozen vegetables	48.9	31.2	27.5
Frozen fruit juices	49.7	35.7	26.9
Bakery products	53.9	41.8	89.3
Dairy products	50.2	29.5	5.3
Coffee	35.8	9.5	5.3
Bacon	44.8	31.1	33.5
Wieners	33.2	12.3	31.7
Wholesale sales (millions)	$4,329.8	$558.9	$343.8

Source: National Commission on Food Marketing, "Private Label Products in Food Retailing. Case Studies of the Dynamics of Brand Competition," *Special Studies In Food Marketing,* Technical Study No. 10, Washington, D.C., June 1966, pp. 20-21.

The retail stores surveyed had a sales volume of $4.3 billion, at wholesale prices, in the categories covered. Private brands accounted for at least a quarter of the sales in each category, exceeded 50% of total sales for bakery products and dairy products, and were just under that proportion for frozen vegetables and frozen fruit juices. A large pro-

---

Inc., White Sulphur Springs, West Virginia, June 14, 15, 16, 1965, (mimeo), pp. 5-17. See also "The Customer and the Competition," *This Week Magazine 11th Biennial Grocery and Drug Study,* 1965, p. 60.

48 The Commission reported that for breakfast cereals "private labels never have been highly successful." "Food From Farmer to Consumer," *op. cit.,* p. 67.

portion of the sales of the two groups of wholesalers also were private brands, but their relative importance was a little lower than for the retail group. Each group also sold a small amount of unadvertised brands.[49]

The Commission also surveyed the *proportion of retailers* carrying private labels for 12 groups of *nonfood products*. (See Table III-2)

Table III-2
Proportion of Retailers Carrying Private Labels in 12 Nonfood Categories, 1965

	Percent
Laundry detergents	78
Laundry supplies	58
Paper products	55
Household supplies	50
Soft drinks	47
Pet foods	38
Soaps	31
Health and beauty aids	31
Candy	26
Housewares	16
Tobacco products	3
Beverage powders	2

Source: "Special Studies In Food Marketing," *op. cit.,* p. 45.

These data show that many stores sell nonfood products with private labels but do not indicate the relative importance of sales. It was reported that "The larger retailers most frequently carried a private label—all the larger retailers had private label laundry detergents and paper products. Laundry detergents was the most popular category for private labels."[50]

It seems clear that for many products, national brands meet very intense competition from private brands. This competition can be very effective, particularly when the retailer builds up a reputation for quality, as many food chains do, and gives preferred shelf space to his own brands.

49 For voluntary group wholesalers, the proportion of sales ranged from 0.3% (coffee) to 9.9% (wieners) and for cooperative group wholesalers from 0.5% (coffee) to 12.9% (bacon). "Special Studies In Food Marketing," *op. cit.,* pp. 20-21.

50 *Ibid.,* p. 45.

Dynamic Competition: The Record

Barrier to entry should not be considered synonymous with barrier to competition even where new entry may be difficult. Competition may be vigorous and intensive among companies already in the market. This latter development is illustrated by the sharp changes in market shares among such companies. (See Chapter IV.)

Brands backed up by national advertising do not create a position of market power which is so strong that it becomes a guarantee against erosion of market share.[51] In fact, in a number of instances, brands have created no barrier to exit from the market. There have been marked changes in market shares for products in a number of industries with intensive advertising.[52]

Satisfactory data showing changes in market shares are not readily available for all products, and the scattered data that can be obtained vary in quality and in the time periods to which they apply. Every effort has been made to obtain data particularly for products which have the greatest intensity of advertising as measured by the relationship between advertising expenditures and sales.

In some instances, confidential surveys made by A. C. Nielsen and Audits and Surveys have been made available on a coded basis which makes it impossible to identify the

51 An A.C.Nielsen study of 71 dry grocery product classes showed that between 1961 and 1965, there was a *reduction* in the share accounted for by manufacturers' advertised brands as a group in 25 classes and an increase in 46 classes. James O. Peckham, "Manufacturers' Advertised Brands: The Consumer's Choice," An Address Before the Grocery Manufacturers of America, Inc., New York, November 9, 1965, p. 9. Since the Nielsen study treated all manufacturers' brands as a group, it is probable that if it had been confined only to brands available in 1961, it would have shown a larger number of product classes with declining shares.

52 There is some evidence that changing market shares also have developed in industries with heavy advertising expenditures in England. Illustrations include: toilet paper (p.84), razor blades (pp. 93-95), toothpaste (p. 98), detergents (p. 147), instant coffee (p. 173), margarine (p. 273), biscuits (p. 276), and cake mixes (p.281). Ralph Harris and Arthur Seldon, *Advertising In Action,* The Institute of Economic Affairs, Hutchinson & Co., London, England, 1962.

names of products. This is not a barrier to the use of such data, since the main interest is in what has happened in the marketplace rather than in the identity of the competitors affected.[53]

It must be recognized that estimates from trade sources may not yield the precise percentage shares which actually prevail. However, while there may be some errors in the changes shown in market shares over time, there can be little question concerning the *fact* of change.

Nevertheless, it would be desirable to have available more complete data on advertising-sales ratios and market shares for a longer list of products on a continuing basis. Such data, both for brands and for firms, would shed considerable light on the results of competitive pressures.

TELSER STUDY

Professor Telser of the University of Chicago analyzed the market shares of 28 leading brands of foods, 15 toiletries and cosmetics, and 9 soaps, waxes, and polishes in the Milwaukee area between 1948 and 1959. He postulated, "If advertising succeeds in sheltering a firm's products from competitive inroads, this should be reflected in more stable market shares of the more advertised goods." He compared the experience of toiletries and cosmetics and soap, "most intensively advertised commodity classes," with foods, "a much less intensively advertised class." The basic data were consumer interviews compiled annually by the *Milwaukee Journal.*[54]

The following changes took place in the average share of sales of *the 1948 leading brands:*[55]

53 It is recognized that such data cannot be used to determine whether new brands or greater success with existing brands has replaced another brand sold by the same company.

54 These surveys report the percentage of "users" who name the various brands they "typically buy." Although the resulting "recalled-brand shares" are "highly correlated" with actual market shares, Professor Telser found that the ". . . biases of recalled shares tend to overstate the level and stability of the shares of more advertised goods relative to less advertised goods." Telser, *op. cit.,* p. 547.

55 *Ibid.,* p. 550.

For 28 foods, from 42.6% in 1948 to 34.1% in 1959.

For 9 soaps, waxes, and polishes from 38.9% in 1948 to 29.9% in 1959.

For 15 toiletries and cosmetics, from 35.5% in 1948 to 25.4% in 1959.

In each category, *new leading brands* had developed as the following data show:

For foods, the 1959 leading brands averaged 42.2% as compared with 34.1% for the 1948 leading brands in 1959.

For soaps, waxes, and polishes, the 1959 leading brands averaged 40.3% as compared with 29.9% for the 1948 leading brands in 1959.

For toiletries and cosmetics, the 1959 leading brands averaged 30.1% as compared with 25.4% for the 1948 leading brands in 1959.

A similar picture emerged for the *four leading brands.* The following changes took place in the *average share per brand.*[56]

For foods from 20.7% in 1948 to 16.4% in 1959.

For soaps, waxes, and polishes from 16.8% in 1948 to 11.4% in 1959.

For toiletries and cosmetics, from 17.8% in 1948 to 12.3% in 1959.

Since each of the totals represents averages covering 9 to 28 products, it is evident that these data do not show that every product recorded comparable changes. The average declines of one-fifth to one-third in the shares of the 1948 leading brands between 1948 and 1959, however, suggest that few brands were exempt from this erosion of position. And since the recalled brand shares were believed to be more stable than actual market shares, the shifts in the marketplace were probably greater than shown by these data.

Professor Telser drew the following conclusions from his study:

56 *Ibid.,* p. 549.

These results refute the view that advertising stabilizes market shares. I explain these findings on the ground that there is more frequent introduction of new toiletries and cosmetics than of new food items. *Despite heavier advertising, brands of cosmetics and toiletries are unable to maintain consumer acceptance for as long a time as branded food products.*

. . . *the relatively intensive advertising of certain goods is associated with high turnover of brands within the product class.* Although this does not imply a correspondingly high turnover of the firms that sell these brands, there is probably some association between the two. *Contrary to popular belief, there may well be more entry and competition among the firms that produce heavily advertised goods.*[57]*(Italics added.)*

DRUGS

There have been marked increases in the number of firms and for many drug products. (See Appendix Tables E-2 and E-3.) For example, the *number of firms* producing multiple vitamins increased from 45 to 80 between 1953 and 1959 and those producing laxatives from 28 to 52. Clearly, the barriers to entry were low. (See Chart III-1.)

Professor James W. McKie has pointed out that for drug products "In all cases it is clear that the period of 'dominance' of any one product is short—four or five years at most—and that a firm which fails to bring out improvements or new substitutes will find its share of the market rapidly passing to others."[58]

The extent to which new companies entered the steroid field between 1950 and 1958 has been dramatically illustrated by John T. Connor, then president of Merck & Company (See Chart III-2.) Although Merck introduced cortone and had 100% of the market in 1950, by 1954 its share had fallen to 26.8% while by 1956 it was down to 7.7% (cortone 3.2%

57 *Ibid.,* p. 550

58 "Administered Prices," *Hearings before the Senate Subcommittee on Antitrust and Monopoly,* 86th Cong., 2nd Sess., 1960, Part 17, p. 9954.

plus hydrocortone 4.5%). Mr. Connor reported that in 1959, there were 29 companies selling steroid products.[59] The Kefauver Hearings are replete with other illustrations of products with similar patterns of entry.[60]

CHART III-1

Number of Firms for Selected Drug Products, 1953 and 1959

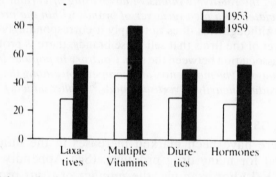

Although the drug industry has relatively high advertising and promotion costs, Professor William S. Comanor, of Harvard University found that:

> ... the rapid rate of product introduction has developed into vigorous product competition. New products have replaced older ones, and in this process the *ranking of the leading firms* in particular therapeutic markets *has changed frequently. In only nine out of twenty such markets did the same firm persist as the leading firm between 1951 and 1960; and in most cases the same five firms did not retain completely the leading positions.* While past position tends to be an advantage in determining present market shares, it is not of crucial significance, and *the measure of market control derived from a single product appears to be limited to a relatively short period of time.*[61] *(Italics added)*

59 *Ibid.*, Part 14, pp. 8029-30.
60 *Ibid.*, Parts 14 to 17.
61 William S. Comanor, "Research and Competitive Product Differentiation in the Pharmaceutical Industry in the United States," *Economica*, November 1964, p. 377.

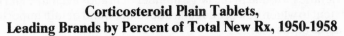

CHART III-2
Corticosteroid Plain Tablets,
Leading Brands by Percent of Total New Rx, 1950-1958

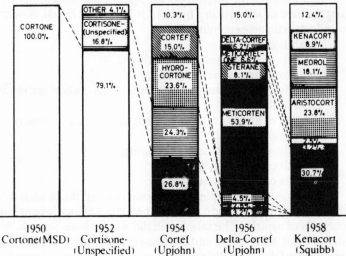

1950	1952	1954	1956	1958
Cortone(MSD)	Cortisone- (Unspecified)	Cortef (Upjohn) Hydrocortone (MSD)	Delta-Cortef (Upjohn) Meticortel- one (Schering) Sterane (Pfizer) Medicorten (Schering)	Kenacort (Squibb) Medrol (Upjohn) Aristocort (Lederle)

He also called attention to " . . . the high turnover among leading firms and the vigorous product competition within these markets."[62]

For proprietary drugs, the most heavily advertised to the consumers, competition is a fact of life about which company officials are painfully aware. Substitute products are frequently offered to the public. When the consumer buys these products, the consequences are felt immediately by other producers, who find that their sales volume stops increasing or begins to decrease.[63]

A significant test of the competitive pressures for pro-

62 *Ibid.,* p.379.
63 Adapted from Jules Backman, "Economics of Proprietary Drugs," *Annals of The New York Academy of Sciences,* July 14, 1965, pp. 896-99.

prietaries is found in the large number of brands available and the extent to which new products are developed and obtain important shares of the market.

Some idea of the intensity of competition is indicated by the compilation of advertising by brands by *Drug Trade News*.[64] It found advertising expenditures for:

- 22 brands of vitamins;
- 78 brands of cough and cold products;
- 17 brands of headache remedies;
- 59 brands of ointments, liniments, and other external medication;
- 33 brands of antacids, laxatives, and stomach sweeteners;
- 12 brands of tonics;
- 6 brands of sedatives and stimulants;
- 6 brands of calorie products;
- 13 brands of other dietary aids.

This was not a complete tabulation of all of the brands available. For example, included in the 17 headache remedies were only 5 brands of aspirin. The tabulation did not include Squibb, Norwich, Rexall, McKesson, and the numerous private brands that are readily available. Nor did the tabulation include the many ethical products that often compete with proprietaries.

To determine the number of brands available to consumers, Audits and Surveys Company made a study in the fall of 1964 of representative drug stores in 10 cities throughout the United States. For each city the number of brands offered was determined for a chain drugstore and independent store in the downtown area, and for a neighborhood store. In addition, the total numbers of brands, after elimination of duplications, were determined for the three stores in each city. The average results are shown in Table III-3.

The average number of brands available ranges between:

- 9 for eye lotions and 21 for cough syrups in chain drug stores;
- 9 for nose drops and 24 for cough syrups in independent drug stores;
- 6 for nose drops and 18 for cough syrups in neighborhood stores.

Every brand is not carried by every store in a city. Thus, the total number of brands available in a community is greater

64 *Drug Trade News,* June 22, 1964.

than those offered in any one type of store. For example, an average of 20 headache remedies was available per city for three stores, although the average number offered by chain stores was 15, by independent stores, 13, and by neighborhood stores, 11.

Table III-3
Average Number of Brands Offered in 10 Chain Drug Stores, 10 Independent Drug Stores, and 10 Neighborhood Stores in 10 Cities (Fall, 1964)

	Average Unduplicated Number Per City	Chain	Independent	Neighborhood
Headache remedies	20	15	13	11
Stomach remedies	31	19	18	16
Cough syrups	35	21	24	18
Nose drops	14	10	9	6
Nasal spray	18	11	11	8
Eye lotions	14	9	10	7
Cold tablets	28	15	15	15
Dentures	16	11	11	10
Oral antiseptics	18	13	12	12
Throat lozenges	21	14	13	11
Laxatives	30	18	21	15
Acne remedies	23	14	14	8

Note: One representative chain drug store, one independent drug store in the downtown area, and one neighborhood drug store were surveyed in each of the following 10 cities: Phoenix; Baltimore; Los Angeles; Oklahoma City; Portland, Maine; Columbus, Ohio; Kansas City, Missouri; Chicago; Miami; and New York. Source: Audits and Surveys Company.

Many competing brands have been introduced during recent years. The following are illustrative:

Acne Remedies:	Stri-Dex, Tackle, Mennen Face Conditioner, and Date-Line Acne Blemish Care.
Cold Tablets:	Dristan, Vicks Tri-Span, Contac, Clinicin, and Allarest.
Cough Syrups:	Vicks Formula 44, Arrestin, and Dristan.
Denture Adhesive:	Ora-Fix, Fixodent.

Eye Lotions: Visine Eye Drops.
Headache Remedies: Excedrin, Vanquish,
                      Measurin, and cope.
Throat Lozenges: Isodettes and Micrin.
Stomach Remedies: Rolaids.

The entry of these products into their respective markets has reflected the dynamic nature of competition in the drug industry.

GROCERY PRODUCTS

The enormous increase in the number of grocery items offered for sale between 1950 and 1963 is shown below:[65] (See Chart III-3)

	No. of Items 1950	1963	Percent Increase
Soaps, detergents	65	200	207.7
Frozen foods	121	350	189.2
Paper products	52	145	178.8
Baking mixes, flour	84	200	138.0
Candy, gum, nuts	150	275	83.3
Beverages	133	210	57.9
Health and beauty aids	250	351	40.4
Pet foods	58	81	39.7

The importance of new products to leading advertisers is often very high. One study reported that " . . . products introduced since 1953 represent 70% of P & G's sales in 1963, 50% of S. C. Johnson's, 90% of Alberto-Culver's, 60% of Bristol-Myers, 33% of Campbell Soup's and 20% of General Foods'." This growth appropriately was described as a "product explosion."[66] The large number of products available in most grocery stores is evident to any shopper.[67]

65 *Progressive Grocer,* April 1965, p. 104.

66 "The Customer and the Competition," *This Week Magazine 11th Biennial Grocery and Drug Study,* 1965, pp. 14-15.

67 A survey of metropolitan Chicago showed the following numbers of brands stocked: ". . . for coffee, 10 in chain stores and 9 in independents: for canned peas, 8 in chain stores and 4 in independents; for toilet soap, 14 in chain stores and 15 in independents; and for scouring cleanser, 7 in chain stores and 7 in independents." This survey took place in the early 1950's; today the number of brands stocked would undoubtedly be greater. Ross M. Cunningham, "Brand Loyalty-What, Where, How Much?" *Harvard Business Review,* January-February 1956, p. 122.

CHART III-3
Number of Grocer Items Offered for Sale, 1950 and 1963

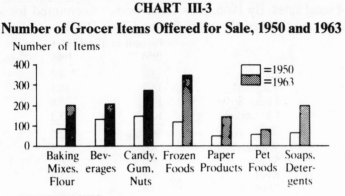

DEODORANTS

Many deodorants are heavily advertised. Nevertheless, it is a matter of common observation that new brands are constantly appearing and new forms of application have been developed. We have come a long way from the period when the main form of protection was a bath with Lifebuoy Soap. A survey of the brands available in 1964 revealed the following:

Types of Deodorants	Number of Products
Solid	94
Aerated and liquid	88
Stick	81
Cream in dispenser applicator	35
Roll on	73
Spray type	73
Aerosol powder	10
Deodorant pads	5
TOTAL	459

This total is a rough approximation. It does not include many unimportant brands and private brands nor does it include soaps. There are duplications among the different types because some brands are available in several different forms. It seems clear, however, the consumer has such a wide variety of alternative products available that it is unnecessary to "have his best friend tell him."

CIGARETTES

In 1956, four brands of cigarettes accounted for 56.1%

of total sales. By 1966, these four brands accounted for less than one-third of the market (see Chart III-4):

	Percent of Total Sales	
	1956	**1966**
Camel	17.6	9.4
Pall Mall	14.2	14.1
Lucky Strike	14.1	5.6
Chesterfield	10.2	3.2
Total	56.1	32.3
Winston	8.6	14.2
Salem	1.0	8.7
Kent	0.9	5.7
Marlboro	3.6	5.6

Two of the four brands were no longer in the Big Four; Lucky Strike was tied for fifth place with a market share less

CHART III-4
Changing Shares of Cigarettes by Brands, 1956 and 1966

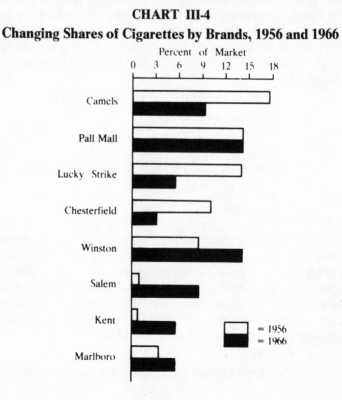

than half as large as in 1956 and Chesterfield fell to thirteenth place when its market share declined by two-thirds. Winston and Salem increased their market shares significantly to join the Big Four. Camel dropped from first to third as its market share fell from 17.6% to 9.4%. These trends were undoubtedly affected by the various studies claiming a link to cancer. Yet, despite these charges two of the largest sellers were not filter brands.[68] Despite heavy advertising some new brands have not been too successful.[69]

SOAPS AND DETERGENTS

This market has been characterized by the introduction of many new products, particularly the shift from soaps to detergents, and dramatic changes in market shares. Companies have not been able to transfer sales to a new product merely by continuing a familiar brand name. Thus, in 1948 Rinso Soap (Lever) accounted for 17.7% of the total sales of these products. The ratio fell steadily to 3% in 1954 when Rinso Blue was made available. Rinso Blue could not recover the lost market share; in 1960 it accounted for about 3%.[70]

Similarly, Super Suds Soap (Colgate), which had 10.5% of the market in 1948, declined to 1% in 1953 and only a nominal share in succeeding years. Super Suds synthetic failed to achieve as much as 1% of the market in any year. Oxydol soap (Procter and Gamble), which fell from 17.6% in 1948 to a nominal share by 1953, was able to recover part of this market with Oxydol synthetic, which had 5.3% of the market in 1960. On the other hand, Tide (Procter and Gamble) increased from 13.1% in 1948 to 35.0% in 1952. Its share was

68 John C. Maxwell, Jr., "Cigarette Marketing: What's Ahead?" *Printers' Ink,* February 14, 1964, p. 28 and "Winston Passes Pall Mall To Become Number One," *Printers' Ink,* December 9, 1966, p. 11.

69 For example, American Tobacco spent large sums advertising Hit Parade, a filter-tip cigarette, but it was not successful. Schorr, *op. cit.,* pp. 116-17.

70 The experience between 1948 and 1960 was reported in an antitrust case involving Lever Brothers when it acquired All from Monsanto. Data reproduced in *Advertising Age,* January 28, 1963, p. 60.

eroded in the following years to 28.3% in 1960 and an estimated 15.0% in 1965.[71]

The toilet soap product industry has seen similar dramatic changes. In 1959, Lever and Procter and Gamble were believed to account for about 52% of total sales in the United States. Then Dial, a product of Armour & Company not previously in the consumer soap business, began to grow in importance. In the following six years Dial made spectacular progress and became the largest-selling brand in the United States;[72] the Procter & Gamble and Lever share declined to about 45% and their total sales fell by more than one million cases.

HAIR PREPARATIONS

The hair-preparations industry has been expanding very rapidly, in large measure as a result of the steady flow of new products and new methods of applying older ones.[73] For example, the hair-spray market was estimated to have expanded from $2 million in 1961 to $168 million three years later. It has been reported that:

> . . . the newcomers that have made their way into test markets or onto national distribution in 1964 include: Five Minute Hair Color, Born Blonde Color toner (Clairol), Coloratura color shampoo (Dorothy Grey); Polycolor, Foam Sparkle (Richard Hudnut) . . . Aqua Net hair spray for men (Rayette); Sheer Glory Hair Spray in four colors (Alberto-Culver); Respond Hair Spray (Colgate-Palmolive); Hidden Magic hair spray (P & G); Super Natural Hair Spray (Revlon); Coiffure Italienne high lighting and setting gel (Max Factor); Brilliantine men's

71 Bold (P&G), a new detergent introduced early in 1965, had an estimated 2.7% by the end of that year. In 1966, its proportion rose to over 6% and it ranked second in the market behind Tide. *Advertising Age,* August 29, 1966, p. 180. See also *Sales Management,* October 15, 1966, p. 51.

72 It has been estimated that Dial accounted for 19% of the dollar volume of toilet soaps. *Advertising Age,* August 29, 1966, p. 64.

73 For example, Alberto-Culver Co., whose products are chiefly in the hair care field, increased its sales from $1.5 million in 1956 to $102 million in 1964. Standard and Poor, *Standard Corporation Descriptions, A-B,* June-July 1966, p. 7649.

hair dressing gel (Yardley); Sentry shampoo for men (Bristol Myers).[74]

This is quite a line up for a single year and gives some idea of the growing competition both for men's and women's hair preparations. According to the U. S. Bureau of the Census, the four largest companies accounted for 42% of total shipments in 1963 or 9 percentages *lower* than the ratio of 51% in 1954.[75]

This industry provides an interesting illustration of how competition from a foreign company may affect U.S. market shares. Thus, Beecham's Brylcream, a hair dressing, was initially marketed in Great Britain in 1928. It was introduced in this country in 1936 with little promotion. By 1954 it accounted for only 3.5% of the total U.S. market. Four years later, Brylcream had 11% of the market. By 1961, *Advertising Age* described it as "the world's leading hair dressing."[76]

DENTIFRICES

The market for dentifrices has been considerably expanded. Sales were estimated at $178.3 million in 1956, $224.8 million in 1960, and $281.6 million in 1965. During this period, sales of regular toothpaste declined in importance both relatively and absolutely while the newly developed fluorides account for about one-third of this rapidly growing market; whiteners also have increased in importance.[77]

Table III-4
Five Leading Dentifrice Brand Positions, 1946-1965

Ranking of Brands	1946	1951	1956	1961	1965
First	A	A	A	A	I
Second	B	C	H	I	A
Third	C	B	I	H	H
Fourth	D	F	C	C	J
Fifth	E	G	B	B	C

Source: A. C. Nielsen Food-Drug Index

74 Lydia Wallack, "Hair Preparations Hit New Peaks," *Printers' Ink,* December 4, 1964, pp. 46-47.

75 "Concentration Ratios In Manufacturing Industry, 1963," *op. cit.,* p. 183

76 *Advertising Age,* August 29, 1966, p. 69.

77 These estimates were derived from "Toothpaste Squeeze Is TV

Table III-4 shows the changes in ranking and the market shares for the five leading brands of dentifrices since 1946 at five-year intervals.

The fourth and fifth largest brands in 1946 were not among the five largest in 1951. By 1956, the second and third largest sellers in 1951 had fallen to fourth and fifth place and two new brands were among the Big Five. In 1965, Brand A, the 1951 leader, was in second place, and Brand I, not among the 1951 Big Five, was in first place. Brands B, F, and G were no longer in the Big Five in 1965, and Brand J joined the group for the first time. Clearly, dramatic changes have taken place in market shares.[78]

That large advertising expenditures do not assure the success of a brand is indicated by Procter & Gamble's experience with Teel, a liquid dentifrice. After successful test-marketing in competition with the leading dentifrices, pastes and powders, Teel was offered nationally in the Spring of 1939 with powerful introductory advertising and promotion which included wide-scale sampling of urban homes. Although Teel's initial sales in the national market were quite encouraging, signs of weakness began to be evident toward the end of its first national year. Following a plateau period, during which advertising was maintained, its share dwindled substantially. Advertising was reduced, then discontinued, and the brand eventually disappeared from the market.[79]

READY-TO-EAT CEREALS

Although the ready-to-eat cereal market has been dominated by a small number of companies,[80] brand shares have changed over time. Table III-5 shows the ranking of the five

---

Bonanza," *Sponsor,* October 31, 1966, pp. 27-38.

78 Changing market shares also are reported for Great Britain. Macleans' share was 17.4% in 1960, 19.3% in 1962, 17.6% in 1963, and 20.1% in 1964. Colgate and Gibbs fluoridated toothpastes were introduced in 1962 and a year later were estimated to account for 8.6% and 11.9% of the total accounted for by the six leading brands. *Ibid.,* pp. 32-33.

79 P & G White naphtha laundry soap (bar) is another illustration of a former leading product which is now difficult to obtain.

80 In 1964, six large manufacturers "held almost all the breakfast

largest brands at five-year intervals since 1941.

Table III-5
First Five Brand Leaders in Ready-to-Eat Cereal Market, 1941-1965

Ranking of Brands	1941	1946	1951	1956	1961	1965
First	A	A	A	A	A	A
Second	B	B	G	G	C	G
Third	C	C	B	F	F	F
Fourth	D	F	F	H	H	H
Fifth	E	G	C	B	B	I

Source: A. C. Nielsen, Food Index

Although Brand A has held first place throughout the period, Brand B, in second place in 1941, fell to third place in 1951 and to fifth place in 1956; it was not among the five leading brands in 1965. The first four brands held their respective ranks in 1956, 1961, and 1965. Brand I appears on the list in 1965. Unfortunately, data were not available showing the percentage shares of each brand.

Table III-6
Market Shares by Brand of Ready-to-Eat Cereals, 1962 and 1965

Brand	Maker	1962	1965
		(percent)	
Corn Flakes	Kellog	13.5	12.0
Cheerios	General Mills	7.0	8.0
Wheaties	General Mills	5.0	6.5
Rice Krispies	Kellogg	5.5	6.0
Sugar Frosted Flakes	Kellogg	4.0	5.5
Post Toasties	General Foods	5.0	4.5
Shredded Wheat	National Biscuit	5.0	4.0
Special K	Kellogg	3.5	4.0
Cap'n Crunch	Quaker Oats	—	3.0
Wheat Chex	Ralston Purina	2.5	2.0
Raisin Bran	Kellogg	2.0	2.0
Life	Quaker Oats	—	2.0
Total	General Mills	—	2.0
Grape Nuts	General Foods	2.5	1.5
Alpha Bits	General Foods	2.0	1.5

Sources: National Commission on Food Marketing, *Studies of Organization and Competition in Grocery Manufacturing,* Technical Study No. 6, Washington, D.C., p. 81 (for 1962 data) and Robin C. Nelson, "Cereals Snap, Crackle, Sometimes Lay Bombs," *Printers' Ink,* June 24, 1966, p. 22 (for 1965 data).

1965 data compiled by John C. Maxwell, Jr.

Such data are available for 1962 and 1965. (See Table III-6) New brands have been introduced (e.g., Cap'n Crunch, Life, and Total), and older brands have sometimes lost position (e.g. Corn Flakes, Shredded Wheat) while others have increased their market share (e.g. Cheerios, Sugar Frosted Flakes). If data were available for a longer time span, it is probable that more dramatic changes would be shown.

Percapita consumption of ready-to-eat cereals was estimated to have increased as follows from 1950 to 1963.[81]

	1950	1955	1960	1963
		(pounds)		
Regular	3.88	4.13	4.09	4.11
Pre-sweetened	.17	.68	.98	1.21
Nutrition	−	.01	.22	.40
Total	4.05	4.82	5.29	5.72

The dramatic increase of 1.67 pounds per capita was accounted for overwhelmingly by the development of pre-sweetened and high-nutrition types of cereals. These newer products accounted for almost 30% of total sales in 1965 and provided an opportunity for the development and growth of new brands.

According to A. C. Nielsen:[82] "A selected group of long-established ready-to-serve cereals (Kellogg's Corn Flakes,

cereal market"; there were also 52 small firms in this market. The smaller companies "restrict their selling geographically." "Grocery Manufacturing," *op. cit.,* pp. 57-58. Entry into the ready-to-serve market is difficult. It is reported that despite declining volume, the producers of hot cereals "are reluctant to try to translate their knowledge into the more complex field of producing and marketing cold cereals." Capital requirements are high as it is necessary " . . . to invest in multiple production lines because cereal machinery is not altogether flexible among products." *Ibid.,* pp. 75,97.

81 James O. Peckham, "The Impact of Advertising On Turnover," An Address Before the Grocery Manufacturers of America, Inc., New York City, November 10, 1964, Chart 5. See also U.S. Department of Agriculture, Economic Research Service, *Changes in the Market Structure of the Break-fast Foods Industry,* Marketing Research Report No. 623, Washington, D.C., August 1963, pp. 11-12.

82 "Grocery Manufacturing," *op. cit.,* pp. 68, 81.

General Mills' Wheaties, General Foods' Post Toasties, et cetra) shared 83.7 percent of the cereal market in 1954 and only 62.4 percent in 1964 . . . In contrast, a selected group of puffed and extruded cereals shared 8.7 percent of the market in 1954 and 14.3 percent in 1964." The share of the four largest selling brands of ready-to-serve cereals fell from 37.5% in 1954 to 32.4% in 1958 and 29.7% in 1964. These were significant changes in market shares. Robert S. Headen and James W. McKie reported that in 1964, 23.3% of the cold-cereal market was accounted for by new products introduced in the preceding decade.[83]

A strong market position does not give a company the power to assure success for new products. Thus, Kellogg accounts for more than 40% of the cold-cereal market and has held the top spot for years. In 1964, it introduced Corn Flakes with Instant Bananas but withdrew it from the market when the public showed little interest. At the same time, it was reported Post "continues to market Corn Flakes with freeze-dried Strawberries, Blueberries, and Peaches; reports sales exceeding expectations."[84]

NINE CATEGORIES OF PRODUCTS

Audits and Surveys Company, Inc. has made available data on an *unidentified basis* for 9 categories of products (See Table III-7.) These product categories include widely distributed, repeat-purchase products such as razor blades, hair sprays, and shampoos; products with smaller distribution and infrequent purchase such as radios and bathtub caulk; and a specialty product (ammunition).

In order to protect the interests of their clients, these categories are referred to by number (in a random sequence). The data cover the calendar years 1964, 1965, and the first

83 Reproduced in *ibid.,* p. 193. It has been reported that 40% of the 1965 cereal sales of the Kellogg Company consisted of products not on the market prior to 1950. *Advertising Age,* August 29, 1966, p. 142.

84 Robin C. Nelson, "Cereals Snap, Crackle, Sometimes Lay Bombs," *Printers' Ink,* June 24, 1966, p. 29.

six months of 1966. Within each category, the share of each of three brands as a percent of total retail sales is shown.

In every category, individual brands have shown relatively substantial changes in their share of the market in the short span of 1½ years. In category 1, for example, Brand

Table III-7
Brand Shares for Nine Products, 1964-1966

Product	Brand	1964	1965	Jan.-June 1966
1	A	15%	13%	12%
	B	13	16	16
	C	10	9	9
2	A	41	41	40
	B	17	17	14
	C	16	16	18
3	A	14	14	15
	B	14	14	14
	C	9	12	8
4	A	48	46	47
	B	26	26	27
	C	9	12	12
5	A	19	19	21
	B	11	16	18
	C	14	12	12
6	A	16	17	16
	B	8	9	9
	C	7	8	9
7	A	17	18	17
	B	15	14	13
	C	12	12	12
8	A	30	31	27
	B	11	17	21
	C	12	11	10
9	A	33	30	30
	B	27	29	29
	C	14	12	12

Note: The nine categories in alphabetical sequence are: ammunition, ball point pens, bathtub caulk, creme rinses, hair sprays, men's hair preparations, radios, razor blades, and shampoos.

Source: Audits & Surveys Company, Inc.

A was the market kingpin in 1964, but was well behind Brand B in 1966. In categories 2, 5, and 8 the second and third leading brands exchanged places. In category 8, Brand B virtually doubled its share of the market in a year and a half.

For the 27 brands listed, 12 recorded a decline in their share of the market, 11 an increase, and 4 no change. The 1964 largest-selling brand reported a declining share of the market for five products, no change for two and an increase for two. Clearly, even within the short time span of a year and a half, significant changes in market shares developed for this diversified group of products.

Summary and Conclusions

The generalization that large-scale advertising creates a barrier to entry is subject to numerous exceptions. This is not an area where a *per se* rule can be adopted, that is, setting up a percentage of advertising to sales or a dollar volume of advertising as a level which automatically creates a barrier to entry. The situation for each product must be examined together with all the factors which affect entry before deciding that advertising is *the* significant barrier. Capital requirements, lack of production and/or marketing know-how, prospective profits, lack of availability of adequate distribution facilities, failure to have a line of related products—these and other factors play a vital role in the decisions of firms to enter a product market and hence may provide important barriers to entry.

Advertisers have discovered over the years that success in selling requires much more than spending money for advertising. The quality of the product, the effectiveness of the message, the activities of competitors, and the response of consumers can and do play more vital roles than the number of advertising dollars spent. Large financial resources alone do not guarantee the continued acceptance of products nor the ability to introduce new brands successfully.

In some industries, the need for large-scale advertising can contribute to the barriers to entry for some companies. However, it is not a barrier to large companies—either in the industry or outside the industry—which may seek to enter the designated market. Nor does it appear to be a significant barrier for many regional companies already in the industry and desirous of extending their market area.

The proliferation of brands has reflected dynamic competition and has resulted in significant changes in market shares. These developments indicate that the degree of market power which supposedly accompanies product differentiation identified by brand names and implemented by large-scale advertising is much weaker than contended. In this connection, it would be desirable to have available more complete data on advertising-sales ratios and market shares for a longer list of products on a continuing basis.

Undoubtedly, a small company is at a disadvantage in connection with advertising as compared with a large, national company. But such companies face many other formidable barriers to entry. Few companies can start on a national level in our three-quarters-of-a-trillion-dollar economy with or without the money to finance national advertising campaigns. In local and regional markets, advertising costs are much lower than for national campaigns, and hence smaller companies can and do compete with great effectiveness in those areas. Moreover, in such markets small companies often carve out a niche by selling at a lower price than the established national brands. This price differential often is necessary to overcome the reluctance of consumers to buy unfamiliar products or from untested sources.

Actually, practically all markets are an amalgam of elements of monopoly and competition. The fact that a product has a brand is not the totality of the market situation. The possession of the monopoly of a brand is not identical with control of the market. National brands must meet the competition of other national brands, substitute products, private brands, local or regional brands, and products which are sold solely on a price basis. There have been dramatic declines in the shares accounted for by the famous national brands of yesterday. Consumers shift their purchasing in response to price differentials, to more effective advertising, to dissatisfaction with a product, to health scares, and to the desire to experiment. Marked erosions of market shares suggest that the "market power" accompanying the development of national brands often is very weak or nonexistent.

Finally, even where advertising may create a barrier to entry, such a situation does not mean a barrier to competition. That competition is both vigorous and intensive among companies already in the market is clearly apparent from the marked increases in the number of products available and the significant changes that continue to take place in market shares in most industries.

IV

Advertising and Economic Concentration

The combination of power of the purse and barriers to entry are claimed to result in concentration of the market among relatively few firms for products which are advertised intensively. Over time, this concentration allegedly is increased. Thus, Nicholas Kaldor has stated: "That advertising promotes the concentration of economic power cannot reasonably be doubted . . . indeed, if it did not, the whole discussion about the effects of advertising on the efficiency of the economic system would be irrelevant, since only by promoting concentration can advertising affect the working of the economic organization."[1]

According to Assistant Attorney General Donald F. Turner:

> To the extent that larger firms can provide more messages per dollar than their smaller rivals, they will have a strong competitive advantage, and this will be so even if smaller firms spend proportionately as much. *Economies of this sort lead directly to the expansion of larger firms relative to their smaller rivals and thereby to more concentrated market structures.*[2] (*Italics added.*)

1 Kaldor, *op. cit.,* p. 15.   2 Turner, *op. cit.,* p. 3.

Other analysts disagree with these conclusions. Thus, Professor Joel Dean of Columbia University has pointed out:

> The sinister effects of advertising in strengthening a firm's monopoly power have been overemphasized. In many industries the efforts of rivals to differentiate their products have tended to offset each other. Even though the individual firm's selling activity may be designed to enhance market imperfection, *the over-all effect of rival selling activity has been to reduce, to some extent, elements of imperfection* by overcoming those due to consumer ignorance and inconvenience.[3] *(Italics added.)*

How do the facts square with these contentions? Is concentration higher in industries which use advertising intensively than in other industries? What has been happening to market shares in these industries? Before the record is examined, it is of interest to note the limitations of concentration ratios and to indicate briefly the reasons advanced by students of this area for economic concentration where it has developed.

Limitations of Concentration Ratios

Concentration ratios measure the proportion of an industry's economic activity or of a product's volume accounted for by a designated number of large companies. Concentration usually is measured in terms of one or more of the following economic variables; sales or shipments, employment, value added or income originating, and assets (gross or net).[4] The

---

3 Joel Dean, *Managerial Economics,* Prentice-Hall, Inc., Englewood Cliffs, N.J., 1951, pp. 354-55.

4 Each of these bases of measurement is not available for every industry. Thus, shipments may be an unsatisfactory basis for measurement because of the large-scale duplication which occurs when there are heavy shipments between plants in the same classification. See Jesse J. Friedman, *Concentration in American Industry,* Report of the Subcommittee on Antitrust and Monopoly of the Committee on the Judiciary, United States Senate, pursuant to S. Res. 57, Washington, D. C., 1957, p. 193.

higher the proportion accounted for by the largest companies, the greater is alleged to be the control over the market.

It is very difficult to obtain meaningful concentration data for many products. The underlying data are often not very satisfactory. Problems of definition are important. What is an industry? How effectively do the available data delineate the industry in terms of products, firms, or geographic location? In this connection, it has been noted that the Census " . . . classifications were not designed to establish categories necessarily denoting coherent or relevant markets in the true competitive sense, or to provide a basis for measuring market power . . ."[5] Similarly, Professor Edward S. Mason of Harvard has concluded: "Neither uncorrected-census product or census-industry data offer a very good approximation to economic markets. Even if they did, we should not usually be entitled to infer clear-cut conclusions concerning monopoly or competition from data on market shares alone."[6]

The coverage of the data may be too broad to provide a meaningful picture of the market for some products, while it may be too narrow to be significant where there are substitutable products. (e.g., metal cans and glass containers are included in different industries although they are substitutable). Where new products are of expanding importance, concentration ratios based on past experience also must be treated with considerable care.

The geographic coverage also presents a problem. For industries which are essentially local, concentration ratios based on national data will understate the more significant local ratios (e.g., bread). On the other hand, these ratios fail to reflect the impact of imports where they are important (e.g., transistor radios). It is for these reasons that the Bureau of the Census warns that " . . . concentration ratios must be used with an awareness of both their attributes and limitations."[7]

5 *Ibid.,* p. 5.

6 Edward S. Mason, *Economic Concentration and the Monopoly Problem,* Harvard University Press, Cambridge, Mass., 1957, p. 42.

7 *Concentration Ratios in Manufacturing Industry, 1963,* Report

The existence of some degree of concentration is not equivalent to the absence of competition. In this connection, Professor J. P. Miller of Yale University has warned that "The concentration ratio will not, however, distinguish the kinds of competition, i.e., between situations where competition takes the form of rivalry in price and those where it is deflected into sales effort or product differentiation."[8]

And the Council of Economic Advisers has noted: "In many industries, a high concentration of output among a small number of firms is not inconsistent with highly active competition, especially where there is also a fringe of small firms, where entry of new firms is easy, or where there exists active competition from substitute products."[9]

A small number of large firms need not connote limited competition. In many industries the most vigorous and intensive competition takes place between industrial giants, as the experience with cigarettes, detergents, dentifrices, and automobiles has so well demonstrated.

The percentage of a market accounted for by a small number of companies is not the important point. How companies respond to various market stimuli provides the real test of the extent of competition and the significance of concentration ratios. Big Fours in highly concentrated industries may compete among themselves with a vigor and intensity that is as great, if not greater, than the competition found in industries much less concentrated.

This is particularly true in industries in which research

Prepared by the Bureau of the Census for the Subcommittee on Antitrust and Monopoly of the Committee on the Judiciary, United States Senate, Part I, 89th Cong., 2nd Sess., Washington, D.C., 1966, p. XV.

8 John Perry Miller, "Measures of Monopoly Power and Concentration: Their Economic Significance," in *Business Concentration and Price Policy,* Princeton University Press, Princeton, N. J., 1955, pp. 130-31. See also Maxwell R. Conklin and Harold T. Goldstein, "Census Principles of Industry and Product Classification, Manufacturing Industries" in *Ibid.,* pp. 15, 17.

9 *Economic Report of the President, January 1965,* Washington, D.C., 1965, p. 132. See also Irston R. Barnes, "The Merger Act" in *Antitrust In An Expanding Economy,* National Industrial Conference Board, New York, 1962, p. 31.

yields a large flow of new products. As Professor Louis B. Schwartz of the University of Pennsylvania has noted: " . . . a very high market share would not necessarily evidence real power if new products or producers were rapidly entering the field and displacing the front-runner."[10] This is the situation for many intensively advertised products as is indicated in Chapter III and later in this chapter.

Finally, the combination of companies comprising the Big Four or Big Eight may vary for the different products in an industry and for the same product over time. Clearly, the interpretation of concentration ratios must be handled with great care. Even when the basic data are homogeneous and statistically accurate, their significance is subject to considerable dispute. This problem is compounded when the underlying data do not provide an accurate portrayal of the market facts.

Proposed Measures of High Concentration

There is no objective way to determine the dividing line between a concentrated and an unconcentrated industry. When such a line is drawn, it usually involves a subjective valuation rather than one based on objective scientific determination.

Proposed dividing lines include:

Kaysen and Turner: They established two combinations for what they call "a structurally oligopolistic market." "In what we call Type One structural oligopoly, the first eight firms have at least 50 percent of total market sales and the first twenty firms have at least 75 percent of total market sales . . . Type Two structural oligopoly is defined by a market share of 33 percent for the eight largest sellers, with the rest of the market relatively unconcentrated."[11] Professor

10 Louis B. Schwartz, "Monopoly. Monopolizing and Concentration of Market Power: A Proposal," in *Perspectives on Antitrust Policy,* edited by Almarin Phillips, Princeton UniversityPress, Princeton, N. J., 1965, p. 122.

11 Carl Kaysen and Donald F. Turner, *Antitrust Policy,* Harvard

Kaysen later testified in connection with these dividing lines that " . . . this is a classification of structure, not a determination of monopoly or competition."[12]

Bain: "High concentration" is considered to be 70% or more of the market supplied by the largest 8 sellers.[13]

Stigler: "Unconcentrated industries meet one of two conditions: (1) the market is national, and the concentration ratio [four largest firms] is less than 50 percent; (2) the market is regional, and the concentration is less than 20 percent."[14]

These proposed standards for high concentration provide a considerable range. Thus, suggested cut-off points for the Big Eight range from 33% to 70% of the market. This is quite a range. Similarly, the use of the ratio of 50% or more of the market for the Big Four to indicate "high" concentration is considerably higher than the same proportion for the Big Eight although it may be in line with a 70% dividing line for the Big Eight.

Actually, concentration ratios have limited meaning in the absence of detailed studies of a market in terms of all of its competitive characteristics. As is illustrated in the brief case studies cited below, a member of the Big Four in one year has no assurance that it will remain in that position in future years. In fact, the probability is great that over a period of five or ten years, one or more members of the Big Four will be replaced by another company.

University Press, Cambridge, Mass., 1959, p. 27.

12 Testimony of Carl Kaysen in *Economic Concentration,* Hearings Before The Subcommittee on Antitrust and Monopoly of the Committee on the Judiciary, United States Senate, (Part 2) 89th Cong., 1st Sess., Washington, D.C., March 1965, p. 545.

13 Bain, "Industrial Organization," *op. cit.,* p. 413.

14 George J. Stigler, *Capital and Rates of Return in Manufacturing Industries,* National Bureau of Economic Research, Princeton University Press, Princeton, N. J., 1963, p. 57, FN 4. The National Commission on Food Marketing used a similar definition: "High concentration is used to describe a situation in which the four largest firms in a field have more than 50 percent of the business." "Food From Farmer to Consumer," *op. cit.,* p. 93.

Factors Contributing to Economic Concentration

Economists generally have not attributed to intensive advertising a major role in the development of economic concentration. The more important factors which have contributed to the growth in size of American companies have included:[15]

1] Technical forces including the mechanization of industry to obtain the economies of large-scale production, more extensive research, ability to hire better management, better utilization of byproducts, etc.

2] The desire to obtain the economies of large-scale distribution including promotion and advertising, elimination of cross hauling, more efficient system of distribution, market research, etc.

3] The development of national markets as a result of improvements in transportation and communication.

4] Financial forces including the ability to obtain funds on a more favorable basis, use of past losses for tax purposes, etc.[16]

The ability to attain the goal of large size has been facilitated by:

1] The development of the corporate form which made it possible to obtain the required large financial resources.[17]

2] Mergers.

3] The patent system.

4] Control over supplies of strategic resources.

5] Policies of innovation and market development.[18]

Professor Neil H. Borden sought to determine the effect of advertising on economic concentration. He concluded:

In certain industries advertising has been employed to

15 See, for example, Bain, *op. cit.,* Ch. 5; Dudley F. Pegrum, *Public Regulation of Business,* Richard D. Irwin, Homewood, Ill., 1959, pp. 94-98; George W. Stocking and Myron W. Watkins, *Monopoly and Free Enterprise,* Twentieth Century Fund, New York, 1951, Ch. 3; Kaplan, *op. cit., passim.*

16 Brink and Kelley, *op. cit.,* p. 300.

17 See Vernon A. Mund, *Government and Business,* Fourth Edition, Harper & Row, New York, 1965, pp. 45, 62.

18 Miller, *op. cit.,* pp. 132-33.

bring concentration of demand upon a few suppliers. In bringing concentration of demand it has probably had some, though not strong influence in keeping down the number of suppliers . . .

In some of the industries studied, in which there is concentration of supply, the leading companies are large advertisers, but *forces other than advertising have an important bearing on the degree of concentration* . . . [in the] cigarette . . . automobile, refrigerator and petroleum industries . . .

Concentration is determined by numerous forces other than advertising . . .[19] *(Italics added.)*

Bigness and economic concentration are not necessarily identical, although there is a tendency for the largest companies to be found in the industries with higher degrees of concentration. Moreover, it is important to distinguish between cause and effect. Students of this problem have concluded that *companies seek to become large in order to obtain the economies of large-scale promotion, not that sales promotion or advertising create economic concentration.* In this connection, Professor Joe S. Bain has stated:

Parallel to the drive for productive efficiency, there is a drive on the part of firms in some industries (largely consumer-goods industries) *to develop scales which are most effective or profitable for sales promotion.* Operation of this force may lead to the development of larger firms and higher degrees of seller concentration than would be required for technological reasons alone — and also to more vertical integration. *(Italics added.)*[20]

And Professors Brink and Kelley of the University of Pennsylvania have observed that: "Ability to attract demand to the resultant oligopoly's brand is less crucial than ability to form the oligopoly in the first place."[21]

It is important to keep this cause and effect relationship in proper perspective when one seeks to evaluate the relationship between the intensity of advertising and economic concentration.

19 Borden, "The Economic Effects of Advertising," *op. cit.,* pp. 859, 860, 863.

20 Bain, *op. cit.,* pp. 182-83; see also 172-73.

21 Brink and Kelley, *op. cit.,* p. 300.

The Record

Some statistical studies have been made of the relationship between the intensity of advertising and economic concentration. One of the most comprehensive analyses of this relationship is that made by Professor Lester G. Telser of the University of Chicago. Studies also have been made by Professor George J. Stigler and by the Federal Reserve Bank of Philadelphia but unlike Telser they have published only their conclusions rather than the data upon which they are based. John Blair of the Senate Subcommittee on Antitrust and Monopoly (Hart Committee) has also published data purporting to find that economic concentration has been the result of TV advertising. These studies are all reviewed or their conclusions reproduced below.

In addition, data available from the Bureau of the Census have been analyzed for 50 industries. Data also have been obtained to show the shares of the largest firms for drug products, beer, cigarettes, ready-to-eat cereals, razor blades, soft drinks, small appliances, and tires for varying time periods. The tire industry has been included to show the pattern of changes in an industry with a relatively low intensity of advertising.

TELSER STUDY [22]

Professor Telser made a statistical analysis of the relationship between the advertising-sales ratio and the proportion of sales accounted for by the four leading producers in 42 consumer goods industries. This study covered three periods: 1947 concentration ratio compared with 1948 advertising-sales ratio, 1954 for both ratios, and 1958 compared with 1957. The Telser data are reproduced in Appendix Table E-4 and Chart IV-1. Although he notes some inadequacies in the data used, Professor Telser found practically no correlation in any of these three years. The coefficients of correlation were an insignificant 0.16 for each of the three years.[23] He concluded:

22 Telser, *op. cit.*, pp. 537-62.　　　23 *Ibid.*, p. 544.

" . . . a 1 percent increase in ratio of advertising to sales is associated with only a 0.08 per cent increase in concentration. Thus, for the forty-two broadly defined consumer product industries at the three-digit level, the *correlation between concentration and advertising is unimpressive.*"[24] (Italics added.)

It is instructive to note that of the 10 industries with the highest advertising ratios, only three (soaps, cigarettes, and cereals) were among the ten with the highest concentration ratios; four were in the lower half of the array for the industries surveyed in 1957-1958.

CHART IV-1

Advertising Outlays as a Percent of Sales, 1957, and Concentration Ratios, 1958, for 41 Consumer Goods Industries

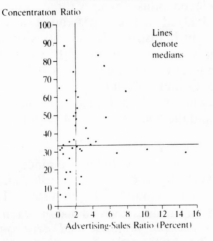

Of the 10 industries with the lowest advertising ratios, 5 were among the 10 industries with the lowest concentration ratios; 2 were among the 10 with the highest concentration ratios.

In 1958, 11 of these industries had a concentration ratio of 50% or higher. These industries with the corresponding

24 *Ibid.*

advertising-sales ratios for 1957 are shown below:[25]

	Concentration Ratio (Percent of Sales by Four Largest Companies)	Advertising (as a Percent of Sales)
Motor vehicles	88.1*	0.9
Cereals	83.0	4.8
Other tobacco (cigarettes)	77.0	5.4
Tires and tubes	74.0	1.9
Sugar	65.1	0.3
Hats	63.2	2.1
Soaps	63.0	7.9
Distilled liquors	60.0	2.4
Motorcycles and bicycles	58.0	1.1
Cigars	54.0	2.4
Carpets	51.4	2.1

    * 1954

Of the eleven industries, only three—cereals, cigarettes, and soaps—had advertising-sales ratios of 4.8% or higher. The other eight industries all had ratios of less than 2.5%. Concentration ratios in excess of 50% were associated with advertising-sales ratios ranging from 0.3% and 0.9% at one extreme to 5.4% and 7.9% at the other.

These data underline the lack of relationship between advertising and the concentration of economic power.

STIGLER STUDY

Professor George J. Stigler examined the relationship between advertising as a percent of sales and the average size of firms in 48 manufacturing industries. He concluded:

Preliminary analysis revealed that *there is no significant relationship between firm size and advertising expenditures* . . . The average ratio of advertising expenditures to sales was 1.97 percent in consumer goods industries and 0.57 percent in producer goods industries, but in neither group was there a significant relationship between the ratio and firm size. (The respective rank correlation coefficients were −.187 and

25 Derived from Telser, *op. cit.,* p. 543. The ratios for advertising have been rounded out.

$-.059$) ... *advertising expenditures have no general tendency to lead to large firms* . . .[26] (Italics added)

FEDERAL RESERVE BANK OF PHILADELPHIA

In 1962, the Federal Reserve Bank of Philadelphia reported:

We decided to look into the relationship between advertising and industrial concentration. The problem was to determine if heavily advertised products tend to be produced by industries that are dominated by a few large firms. *We selected some fourscore common products*—from soft drinks to shoes, from paint to pottery—and determined advertising expenditures as a percentage of sales for each. Next we measured industrial concentration for each product by the percentage of total shipments accounted for by the four largest firms. In about half the cases we had to rely on estimates.

The final step was to determine if a correlation existed between high advertising expenditures and high concentration. We fed the data into a computer which whirred, and blinked, and gave *the verdict, "No significant correlation."*

This does not mean that advertising may not move a product along the scale towards monopoly. It only indicates that heavy advertising is not necessarily associated with those products dominated by only four producers. Obviously, *many factors besides advertising can affect industrial concentration.*[27] *(Italics added.)*

STUDY OF BUREAU OF THE CENSUS DATA

The Bureau of the Census prepared a special study for the Kefauver Committee to show whether the four largest companies in 1947 had retained that position in 1958 and, if they had, whether they retained the same rank.[28] Appendix

26 George J. Stigler, "The Economies of Scale," *The Journal of Law and Economics,* October 1958, pp. 66,71.

27 "Advertising and Charlie Brown," *Business Review,* Federal Reserve Bank of Philadelphia, June 1962, p. 11.

28 *Concentration Ratios in Manufacturing Industry, 1958,* Report prepared by the Bureau of the Census for the Subcommittee on Antitrust and Monopoly of the Committee on the Judiciary, United States Senate, Part II, 87th Cong., 2nd Sess., Washington, D. C., 1962, pp. 469-72.

Table E-5 shows the changes in the share of shipments accounted for by the Big Four in 1947 and in 1958 and the advertising-sales ratio for 1957.

Several limitations inherent in these comparisons should be noted. First, the data for concentration and for advertising are not always available for exactly comparable industries. For example, the table shows separately concentration ratios for three types of appliances as compared with a single ratio for advertising; the concentration ratios in 1947 varied from 39% for refrigeration machinery to 61% for vacuum cleaners. Even more marked is the diverse pattern for biscuits and crackers and bread and related products, both of which are compared with a single figure for bakery advertising. The advertising ratio for professional and scientific equipment is related to the concentration ratio for only one component of the group, namely, photographic equipment.

Secondly, the Census data are for broad industry groupings. The concentration ratios for narrower product groups are usually higher. Comparable data for advertising ratios for narrower product groups also vary from the industry average, but there is no way to determine how they compare with corresponding concentration ratios.

Third, total sales as defined for Census purposes usually include a variety of products, some of which are not products of the industry as defined. As companies branch out into new lines this factor increases in importance. Since there is no reason to believe that the four largest companies in an industry will have exactly the same proportion of their sales accounted for by other products, the comparability of the results is affected.

Fourth, the company concentration ratios fail to show fully the wide changes that take place in the market shares accounted for by particular brands as is noted elsewhere in this study.

Despite these limitations, the data do provide a basis for some broad conclusions. It is evident that significant shifts have developed among the leading firms.

1] For only seven of the 50 industry groups and subgroups listed in Appendix Table E-5 did the four largest companies in 1947 have the same rank in 1958.[29] Only one industry had an advertising-sales ratio in excess of 3% (soap and glycerin, 7.94%).

2] In six industries, the four largest firms remained the same but there was a change in relative rank within the group. None of these industries had an advertising-sales ratio above 3%.

3] In 37 industries, one or more of the four largest companies in 1947 had been replaced by other companies in 1958. 12 of these industries had an advertising-sales ratio in excess of 3%.

Thus, in only 13 out of 50 groups were the 1947 Big Fours able to retain their top position in 1958, and in only one of these industries did the advertising to sales ratio exceed 3%.

The following tabulation summarizes the changes between 1947 and 1958 in the market shares of the four largest firms:

1947 Big Four Change in Shipments, 1947 to 1958 (percent)	Advertising-Sales Ratio			
	Over 5%	3 to 5%	Less than 3%	Total
8 and over	1	3	5	9
3 to 7	2		1	3
2 to -2	1	2	10	13
-3 to -7			8	8
-8 and over	3	2	12	17
	7	7	36	50

In the industries with advertising-sales ratios of more than 3%, about as many 1947 Big Fours recorded a decrease in their share of the total shipments as recorded an increase. However, for industries with advertising ratios of less than 3%, many more Big Fours recorded a decrease rather than

29 From these data, however, it cannot be determined to what extent the shares of each were changed.

an increase in their market shares.[30]

There are seven concentration ratios for industries with advertising expenditures equal to more than 5% of sales: two were above 75%, two were about 50%, and three (including the two with the highest advertising ratios) were less than 30%. These data indicate that relatively high advertising costs are not necessarily accompanied by high concentration ratios. Moreover, in six of these seven industries one or more of the 1947 Big Four had been displaced in 1958 (only in soaps and glycerin was the 1947 Big Four still in that position in 1958).

BLAIR STUDY[31]

Dr. John M. Blair, economist of the Senate Subcommittee on Antitrust and Monopoly, studied the trend of concentration ratios in 36 industries (the four largest companies) in which network TV expenditures were a minimum of $250,000 in 1963. He concluded that between 1947 and 1954 and 1963, concentration ratios increased in 25 out of 36 industries or product classes.[32]

The Blair study includes data for 23 industries and 13 product classes (commodity basis). According to the U. S. Bureau of the Census, "Under the industry approach . . .

30 Comparable data are not available for *identical Big Fours* at this writing for 1958 and 1963. However, data are available for the four largest companies in each year. For industries with advertising-sales ratios in excess of 3%, 6 out of 11 recorded an increase in Big Four concentration and five a decrease. However, out of 11 industries with an advertising-sales ratio under 2%, seven recorded an increase in concentration; two showed no change; and two recorded a decline. Thus, the industries with a lower intensity of advertising had much more widespread increases in concentration than did those with more intensive advertising.

31 Testimony of Dr. John M. Blair, *Hearings on Economic Concentration*, Senate Subcommittee on Antitrust and Monopoly, Washington, D. C., September 12, 1966, (mimeo), 22 pages.

32 If the comparisons for the 36 industries were confined to the changes between 1954 and 1963, 23 recorded increases, 2 showed no changes and 11 had decreases; four of the increases were 4 percentage points or less. Derived from "Concentration Ratios In Manufacturing Industry, 1963," *op. cit.,* pp. 6-37.

the entire shipments of the plants are . . . assigned to a particular industry . . . This will include . . . products classified in other industries as well (secondary products) and miscellaneous receipts and resales." "The commodity basis . . . relates shipments of specific products from the plants of the largest companies to the total shipments of such products . . . Because secondary products are included, the commodity approach more closely approaches the concept of the market."[33]

For 19 of the 23 catagories for which industry data were used, commodity data also were available for 1963. For 14 of these catagories, the concentration ratios on a commodity basis were lower, and for four they were the same as on the industry basis; the ratio was higher on only one category. For 16 of these 19 commodity categories data were available for 1954 and 1963; the increase in concentration was smaller or the decrease was larger for eight categories, higher for four, and the same for four.[34] Thus, within the framework used by Dr. Blair, a somewhat smaller trend toward concentration would have been shown if the more meaningful commodity data had been used where available.

Moreover, the broad composites used sometimes reflect diverse trends for the components. For example, using the industry approach the concentration ratio for perfumes, cosmetics, and other toilet preparations (SIC 2844) rose from 25% in 1954 to 29% in 1958 and 38% in 1963. On a commodity basis the increase was from 29% in 1958 to 33% in 1963 (1954 data not available). About half the television advertising expenditures were for hair preparations (SIC 28443) and shaving preparations (SIC 28441). For hair preparations, the four-firm concentration ratio using the commodity approach declined from 51% in 1954 to 39% in 1958 and then rose to 42% in 1963 or a level 9 percentage points

33 *Ibid.,* pp. XIII-XIV.
34 For 1958 and 1963, data were available for 18 categories on a commodity basis. For eleven categories, there was a smaller increase or a larger decrease in the concentration ratio on a commodity basis; for five there was a larger increase or a smaller decrease.

lower than in 1954. For shaving preparations, the ratio fell from 58% in 1958 to 45% in 1963.[35]

Since total *network TV* expenditures accounted for only 7.8%[36] of total advertising expenditures in 1963, the Blair study claims that a small part of advertising expenditures has had an enormous impact on economic concentration. Gross time billings of $250,000 for an *industry* as a cutoff point for determining a significant amount of network TV advertising is extremely low. This amount of money could buy about 5 hours of prime evening time and hence does not make possible the mounting of a major television campaign.[37] To the extent that more than one company in an industry participates in such expenditures this point is emphasized.

Moreover, the level of advertising expenditures in a single year would appear to be an unsatisfactory basis for determining the significance of changing concentration ratios over the years. Unfortunately, the Blair study does not identify the amount of advertising for each of these industries. However, it should be noted that total expenditures for network TV advertising increased from $422 million in 1954 to $1,025 million in 1963 (Appendix Table A-1). Thus, it would seem to be a fair assumption that industries for which expenditures were close to Blair's cut-off point of $250,000 for 1963 were spending only nominal amounts for this purpose in the preceding decade.

The Blair study is based on dollars of expenditures; it does not show the relative importance of advertising expenditures. Advertising to sales ratios are not publicly available for all of the 25 industries which were shown as recording large increases in economic concentration in this study. Of the 14 industries for which such data are available, the

35 "Concentration Ratios in Manufacturing Industry, 1963," *op. cit.,* pp. 182-83.

36 In addition, spot television accounted for 5.2% of total advertising expenditures in 1963.

37 The annual, cost of a weekly one-hour show on prime television time was estimated to cost $10 million in 1964; this is almost $200,000

ratio was below 4% for eight: household appliances, which is represented by three industries (2.48%), TV sets (1.77%), cutlery (3.28%), flour mills (3.18%), weaving mills, synthetics (0.40%), and motor vehicles (0.74%). Of the 11 industries for which a decrease in the concentration ratios is shown, advertising-sales ratios were available for five; for 4 of these industries the ratio was 4.9% or higher: canned milk (6.0%), ice cream (4.9%), cigarettes (5.28%), and pharmaceutical preparations (9.39%).

Dr. Blair's analysis of these industries overstresses TV advertising and often ignores more significant factors. Thus, the increase in concentration for malt liquors is attributed to the inability of local and regional brewers "to match the national advertising campaigns of the largest firms" and as a result they "went out of business." Dr. Blair does not mention that there has been a large number of mergers in the brewery industry as family enterprises were sold. The resulting creation of national firms provided increased competition.

In connection with the increase in concentration for razor blades it is stated that Gillette "spent as much *per month*" as its two leading competitors spent in a year. However, the study says nothing about Gillett's declining share of the market.[38]

Where concentration *declined,* Dr. Blair attributes this development to "unusual and explainable factors." He refers to the "tendency of the grocery chains to promote private-label or store-brand merchandise" as a key factor causing decreases in concentration for four food products groups. He also recognizes that as a result of the "proliferation of brands, the industry's historical leaders suffered a major setback." For ice cream and the frozen-food industry the decline in concentration is attributed to "the increased utilization of home freezers and dual-purpose refrigerators."

---

a week. "The Structure of Food Manufacturing," *op. cit.,* p. 70, FN 24.

38 Early in 1963, Gillette had 69% of the razor blade market. Two years later its share had fallen to 56%. Patrick J. Kelly, "They're Creeping Up On Giant Gillette," *Printers' Ink,* June 11, 1965, p. 50.

Data compiled by John C. Maxwell, Jr.

Table IV-1
Gross Billings for Television Advertising in 1963 and Four Firm Concentration Ratios, 1954, 1958 and 1963, Ten Commodity Classes

SIC	Gross Billings for TV (1963) (000 omitted)	Four Firm Concentration Ratios 1954	1958	1963	Change in Percentage Points 1954-63	1958-63
		(percent)				
2844 Perfumes, cosmetics and other toilet preparations	$126,368	N.A.	29	33		4
2834 Pharmaceutical preparations	113,861	25	25	22	-3	-3
2841 Soaps and detergents	73,036	N.A.	68	68		0
28443 Hair preparations	53,836	51	39	42	-9	3
37171 Passenger cars and chassis	41,555	98	99	99	1	0
20430 Cereal preparations	28,608	78	80	82	4	2
28423 Specialty cleaning and sanitary products	17,849	N.A.	29	32		3
20423 Dog and cat food	10,913	32	38	42	10	4
28443 Shaving preparations	10,413	N.A.	58	45		-13
3634 Electric housewares and fans (electric razors and toothbrushes)	10,119	N.A.	39	35		-4

N.A. not available

Sources: Concentration Ratios: "Concentration Ratios in Manufacturing Industry, 1963"; gross billings from Stanley Solson of National Broadcasting Company.

But in many instances, an increase in concentration also resulted from unusual and explainable factors. For example, the increase in concentration for household appliances reflects in large measure the entrance of many companies into these industries to take advantage of the early postwar deferred demand. The saturation of this demand, the tendency for retailers to handle a limited number of brands, and the depressed appliances prices[39] in recent years forced many of these companies out of the business and led to increasing concentration.

Personal experience with various makes of cars and the development of strong dealer organizations seem to have been more potent factors in this area than advertising. The disappearance of large numbers of automobile companies before there was any television should not be overlooked either.

For coffee, the study notes that "smaller roasters have been disappearing" because of mergers and because the "advent of instant coffee has lessened the importance of conducting the roasting operation near the marketing area." Thus, factors other than advertising have led to concentration for coffee.

The changes in concentration ratios for the ten commodity classes which had gross TV billings of $10 million or more in 1963 is shown in Table IV-1.

Between 1958 and 1963, five of these categories recorded small increases in concentration ratios and an equal number reported no change or declines.[40] These data do not show any predictable relationship between expenditures for TV advertising and economic concentration. It should also be noted that only three of the ten groups reported a four-firm concentration ratio above 45% in 1963 despite their heavy advertising on TV.

39 According to the U. S. Bureau of Labor Statistics, between 1947 and 1965, retail prices of household appliances *declined* by 26.2%.

40 A study by Stanley Solson of the National Broadcasting Co. of 67 commodity classes which had aggregate network TV gross billings of $645 million in 1963 showed that the four firm concentration ratios had changed as follows from 1954 or 1958 to 1963.

DRUG INDUSTRY

The drug industry had an advertising-sales ratio of 9.39% in 1962. Advertising expenditures are largely for proprietary drugs. The last year for which concentration ratios were officially reported for the drug industry was 1963 when data were compiled for all pharmaceutical preparations and for 10 product classes in this industry. In that year the four largest drug companies accounted for only 22% of the total shipments of drug products as compared with 27% in 1958 and 28% in 1947.[41] However, the four largest companies in an industry or in a specific market are not a static group, as was noted earlier. In relatively short periods, the composition of the group of largest companies often changes.

The Bureau of the Census has reported that for pharmaceutical preparations the composition of the four largest companies changed between 1947 and 1958 so that at least one of the four largest in 1947 no longer was in that group in 1958. Where such a situation develops, the relative share accounted for by a constant group of four companies over time would be less in the terminal year than shown by "Big Four data" based on the four largest companies in each year. The Census reported that between 1947 and 1958 the Big Four of 1947 showed a decline in relative position of 8 percentage points and over.[42] The raw concentration data conceal changes in relative position within a particular market and hence obscure the full effect of competitive forces and the dynamic changes that may be taking place.

BEER INDUSTRY

The beer and malt industry had an advertising-sales ratio

Concentration Ratio	Number of Industries or Commodity Classes	Network TV Expenditures (millions)
Increased	34	$ 312
Decreased	27	242
Unchanged	6	91
	67	$ 645

41 "Concentration Ratios In Manufacturing Industry, 1963," *op. cit.*, p. 19.

42 "Concentration Ratios In Manufacturing Industry, 1958," Part II, *op. cit.*, pp. 470, 472.

of 6.8% in 1962. The U.S. Bureau of the Census has reported that the four largest firms in 1947 accounted for 21% of the total dollar shipments. These companies had increased their share of the market by 3% to 7% by 1958. However, one or more of the companies in the Big Four in 1947 had been replaced by 1958.[43]

The brewery industry has been characterized by many mergers which have affected the relative position of some companies in recent years. Because of the local and regional nature of many markets, national shares have less meaning for this industry than in most other industries with heavily advertised products. Regional brands compete very effectively with national brands. In this connection it has been reported that:

> Lone-Star and its fellow Texan, Pearl (up 3.8%), in fact were so successful in their markets that they forced Carling, a national brand, to close down its new Fort Worth continuous-brewing plant[44]

Competition is so intense that one observer has characterized the beer market as "cannibalistic" and referred to competition in the industry as "savage."[45] The change in rank between 1952 and 1965 of the eight largest companies in 1965 is shown below: (See Chart IV-2.)

Rank in Terms of Barrels Sold

	1952	1957	1962	1965
Anheuser Busch	2	1	1	1
Schlitz	1	2	2	2
Pabst	3	9	3	3
Falstaff	8	3	5	4
Carling	20	6	4	5
Schaefer	7	8	7	6
Ballantine	4	4	6	7
Liebmann-Rheingold	6	7	9	8

43 *Ibid.,* p. 469.

44 Kenneth Ford, "Beer Going Flat Again," *Printers' Ink,* February 11, 1966, p. 16.

45 Kenneth Ford, "What's Missing in Beer Marketing," *Printers' Ink,* November 29, 1963, p. 25.

Anheuser Busch has moved up from 2nd place to 1st place, replacing Schlitz. Carling, which was not in the Big Eight in 1952 entered this group in 1956 and has since remained there as a result of mergers. Hamm was included in this group from 1954 to 1964 but was replaced in 1965. Miller, which was in 5th place in 1952, fell below 8th in 1954 and has not regained its position since then.

CHART IV-2

Changes in the Rank of Beer Companies, Selected Dates, 1952 to 1965

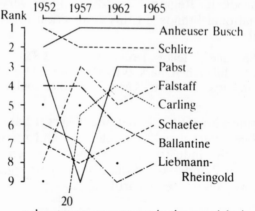

• denotes a company not in the top eight in 1965

Clearly, there has been considerable ferment in the beer industry. However, according to the Bureau of the Census the four largest firms in 1947 had increased their share of total shipments from 21% in 1947 to 28% in 1958 and 34% in 1963. Despite this increase, the total concentration of shipments in the four largest companies was still relatively low.

CIGARETTE INDUSTRY

The tobacco industry had an advertising-sales ratio of 5.28% in 1962. The U.S. Bureau of the Census has reported that the four largest firms accounted for 90% of the total dollar shipments of cigarettes in 1947. The share of the market accounted for by these same four companies declined more than 11 percentage points between 1947 and 1958 and one or more of the companies in the Big Four in earlier years was no longer in that group in 1958.[46]

Dramatic changes have developed in the cigarette market during the postwar years. Despite the cancer scare, which led to the introduction of filter cigarettes and a proliferation of new brands, total consumption increased from 393 billion in 1956 to 529 billion in 1966. American Tobacco, which was the largest company with 31.1% of total sales in 1956 (See Chart IV-3), slipped to second place and has remained in this position. Reynolds took first place in 1958 and has remained in that position although through most of this period its largest selling brand (first Camel, then Winston) was in second place. Reynolds reached its peak share with 34.9% in 1962 and then declined to 32.6% in 1966. Four companies have rotated in third and fourth place:

Brown and Williamson (Viceroy, Kool, Raleigh) was in fourth place in 1956 with 10.9% of the market. It was not among the Big Four from 1958 to 1962. In 1963, it was fourth and in 1964, 1965, and 1966 rose to third; in 1966 it had 14.0% of the market.

Philip Morris (Marlboro, Parliament) became one of the Big Four in 1965 for the first time. Between 1956 and 1964, it accounted for slightly more than 9% of total sales; in 1966 it reached a new high of 10.8%.

Liggett and Myers (L&M, Chesterfield) had the third largest sales in 1956 with 15.4% of the market. Although its share was steadily eroding, it held third place until 1963 when it slipped to fourth place with 10.9%. It was not in the Big Four in 1963, regained fourth place in 1964, and then dropped out again in 1966 when its share fell to 8.8%.

Lorillard (Kent, Newport, Old Gold) has moved into and out of the Big Four. Its share was only 5.4% in 1956 and then rose to 11.8% in 1958 when it reached

46 "Concentration Ratios In Manufacturing Industry, 1958," *op. cit.,* p. 469.

fourth place. It retained this position until 1962 when it rose to third place with 10.9%. However, in 1964, 1965, and 1966 when its share fell below 9.5%, it no longer was among the four largest companies.

The market shares in 1956 and 1966 were estimated to be as follows:[47]

	1956	1966	Percentage Point Change
Reynolds	27.5 %	32.6 %	+5.1
American Tobacco	31.1	24.4	−6.7
Brown and Williamson	10.9	14.0	+3.1
Philip Morris	9.1	10.8	+1.7
P. Lorillard	5.4	9.1	+3.7
Liggett and Myers	15.4	9.0	−6.4

These data portray an industry subject to vigorous competition. Large expenditures for advertising have been accompanied by changing market shares, although the over-all con-

CHART IV-3
Market Shares for Cigarettes, 1956 and 1966
(Percent of Total Sales)

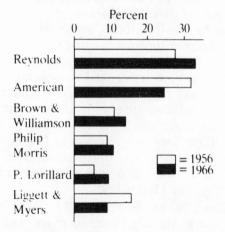

47 The data in this section were derived largely from two articles by John C. Maxwell, Jr. in *Printers' Ink,* February 14, 1964, pp. 26-28 and December 9, 1966, p. 14.

centration of 81.8% of total volume for the four largest companies in 1966 is among the highest in the country.

SOFT DRINK INDUSTRY

Soft drink companies were estimated to spend 7.0% of sales for advertising in 1964.[48] Sales of soft drinks increased from 1,177 million cases in 1954 to 1,861 million cases in 1964. The major companies in this market and their shares[49] are shown below:[50]

	1950	1964
Coca-Cola	48.0%	37.9%
Pepsi-Cola	12.8	19.2
Royal Crown	5.1	10.6
Seven Up	11.6	10.5
Canada Dry	7.4	8.5
Dr. Pepper	2.1	3.0
All other	13.0	10.3
Total	100.0	100.0

The major change in this market has been the decline in the relative position of Coca-Cola from 48% in 1950 and 38% in 1964.[51] The shares of Pepsi-Cola and Royal Crown increased sharply.[52]

Royal Crown, the fifth largest seller with 5.1% of the market in 1950, moved to third place with 10.6% in 1964 largely because of the growing popularity of diet drinks. The extent to which new competitors have entered the diet drink market has been summarized as follows:

"One can no longer mention diet soft drinks such as Royal

48 Ko Ching Shih and C. Ying Shih, *American Soft Drink Industry and the Carbonated Beverage Market,* W. A. Krueger Co., Brookfield, Wis., 1965, p. 122.

49 Shares represent the proportion "controlled-either outright or through franchise arrangements." "The Structure of Food Manufacturing," *op. cit.,* p. 31.

50 Shih and Shih, *op. cit.,* p. 72.

51 Coca-Cola's share of the cola market declined from 63% in 1950 to 44% in 1965. Seven-Up's share of the lemon-lime market fell from 85% in 1950 to 55% in 1965. *Ibid.,* p. 74.

52 Another source estimates the shares in 1964 as 31% for Coca-Cola and 23% for Pepsi-Cola. *Printers' Ink,* April 9, 1965, p. 22.

Data compiled by John C. Maxwell, Jr.

Crown's Diet-Rite, Coca-Cola's Tab or Pepsi-Cola's Diet Pepsi
and say this is the diet drink universe. Nor were these the first
ones. Beverage International Inc., Cott Corp. and Kirsch
Beverages had diet drinks at least 15 to 20 years ago. Now
Coca-Cola has Tab . . ., Sprite lemon-lime, Fresca grapefruit;
Pepsi has Diet Pepsi, Sugar-Free Teem lemon-lime, Patio Flavors. Royal Crown has Diet-Rite Cola and lemon-lime and Dietetic Upper 10 lemon-lime. And there's Seven-Up's Like
lemon-lime, Canada Dry's ten flavors, Diet Dr. Pepper, Beverages International's Diet Crush and Diet Hires root beer,
Cott's Diet Cola and Metri-Cola and Dietetic Squirt."[53]

In addition to the six largest companies, there were
25 others which sold a million cases or more in 1965. Large-
scale advertising did not protect Coca-Cola's market position
nor has the need to advertise prevented smaller companies
from expanding their market shares as is illustrated by the
marked expansion experienced by both Dr. Pepper and Cott.[54]

RAZOR BLADES

Three companies have dominated the sales of razor
blades.[55]

	Early 1963	Early 1965
Gillette	69%	56%
Schick	18	22
American Safety Razor	11	17
Wilkinson	(a)	2
Others	2	3

(a) Not reported separately—included in others

Gillette, the largest company in the industry, is also one
of the largest advertisers.[56] The data show that even in a
two-year period, marked changes in market shares have
taken place. In recent years, the significance of these data

53 Ted Sanchagrin, "Private-Label Soft Drinks Don't Faze Coke and
Pepsi," *Printers' Ink,* April 8, 1966, p. 11.

54 *Ibid.,* and *Printers' Ink,* April 9, 1965, p. 28.

55 Patrick J. Kelly, "They're Creeping up on Giant Gillette," *Printers'
Ink,* June 11, 1965, p. 50. Data compiled by John C. Maxwell, Jr.

56 In 1965, Gillette ranked 19th in dollar advertising expenditures with
such spending equal to 15.3% of sales. *Advertising Age,* August 29, 1966,
p. 44.

has been influenced by two developments: 1] the availability of higher unit cost stainless blades with more shaves per unit and 2] the growth in use of electric shavers.[57] Because of the second factor, razor blades account for a smaller proportion of the total market and the significance of the shares listed is affected accordingly.

READY-TO-EAT CEREALS

Three companies, ranked among top 25 advertisers in terms of dollar expenditures in 1965,[58] accounted for about four-fifths of the cold cereal market.[59]

	1963	1965
Kellogg	43.5%	41.0%
General Mills	20.5	22.0
General Foods	21.0	18.5
Quaker Oats	4.0	7.0
National Biscuit	4.5	5.0
Ralston Purina	3.5	3.5
Others	3.0	3.0
	100.0	100.0

A company generally offers several important brands.[60] It has been reported that entry into this market "over the past two decades has been practically nil."[61] Nevertheless, many new brands are available. "A Chain Store Age survey showed that a typical ($40,000 per week) supermarket in 1964 carried 97 items, brands, and sizes of ready to eat cereals. Nearly half the brands have appeared in less than a decade."[62]

57 "It is estimated that one out of every four shaves is now accomplished with an electric razor." Kelly, *op. cit.,* p. 50.

58 In 1965, advertising expenditures were estimated to be 12.6% of total sales of all products for Kellogg, 9.3% for General Mills, and 8.7% for General Foods. *Advertising Age,* August 29, 1966, p. 44.

59 Robin C. Nelson, "Cereals Snap, Crackle, Sometimes Lay Bombs," *Printers' Ink,* June 24, 1966, p. 22. Data compiled by John C. Maxwell, Jr.

60 For example, Kellogg has Corn Flakes, Rice Krispies, Raisin Bran; General Mills has Cheerios, Wheaties, Total; General Foods has Post Toasties, Alpha Bits, Grape Nuts.

61 "Grocery Manufacturing," *op. cit.,* p. 75.

62 Nelson, *op. cit.,* p. 25.

SOUPS

Campbell Soup has successfully maintained the position of its brand name products which have dominated the wet soup market for many years; in 1965 its proportion was 90%.

The changing shares of the market for *dry soup* are shown below:

	1962	1963	1964	1965
Lipton	47%	50%	56%	57%
Knorr	25	22	14	12
Campbell	16	14	9	8
Wyler's	7	10	13	16

Source: Frank Biancamano, "Campbell Soup Co. Keeps Simmering Along," *Printers' Ink,* November 25, 1966, p. 9 and Patrick J. Kelly, "Campbell Soup's Cup Runneth Over," *Printers' Ink,* September 10, 1965, p. 21. Data compiled by John C. Maxwell, Jr.

Lipton has been the major factor in this market with a steady increase in its market share. Knorr fell from second place in 1962 to third in 1965 while Wyler's advanced from fourth place in 1962 to second in 1965.

Despite its strong position in wet soups, Campbell was able to make little progress in the dry soup market in which its share was 16% in 1962, the year in which it entered this market, and only 8% in 1965. In August· 1966, Campbell Soup announced it was discontinuing its line of Red Kettle dry soup mixes after spending more than $10 million in advertising.[63] Thus, large-scale advertising by a company which was highly successful in marketing wet soups failed to obtain satisfactory market penetration for dry soups.

TIRE INDUSTRY

The U. S. Bureau of the Census has reported that the Big Four companies making tires and tubes accounted for 77% of dollar shipments in 1947 and 74% in 1958.[64] Although the same companies were in the Big Four in both years,

63 *Advertising Age,* August 29, 1966, p. 3.
64 "Concentration Ratios In Manufacturing Industry, 1958," *op. cit.,* p. 470.

there was a change in relative ranking within the group.

Each year *Look* surveyed the tire market to determine what brands of tires are bought for *replacement.* The record for 1958, 1960, and 1964 is shown in Table IV-2.

Table IV-2
Market Share of New Replacement Tires Bought, 1958, 1960, and 1964

	1958 Survey	1960 Survey	1964 Survey
	(percent of total)		
Goodyear	21.5	18.7	19.6
Firestone	18.4	15.3	14.1
Allstate	10.3	13.1	11.1
B. F. Goodrich	6.6	6.1	7.0
Riverside	4.2	6.8	5.6
Atlas	5.0	5.7	5.0
U.S. Rubber	6.8	6.2	4.7
General	2.2	2.8	3.6
All Other	25.0	25.3	29.3
	100.0	100.0	100.0

Source: Look, National Automobile and Tire Survey, 1960, p. 59 and 1964, p. 61.

Goodyear and Firestone have held first and second positions, although there have been declines in their relative shares. Allstate has maintained a fairly steady share in third place. U. S. Rubber dropped from fourth in 1958 to seventh in 1964. This record of relatively small changes in position is of interest because advertising in the tire industry accounts for only about 2% of sales, and hence it is a less intensive advertiser than the industries described earlier.

SMALL APPLIANCES

Data published for several small appliances for 1964 and 1966 show that market shares have been changing, sometimes dramatically. (See Table IV-3.)

For three of the four products (electric knives, food mixers, and portable mixers) the share of the leading company in 1964 had been reduced by 1966. For electric knives, General Electric's share fell from 42% to 24% while Hamilton Beach increased from 12% to 28%. Hamilton Beach also increased its shares sharply for blenders and portable mixers and rose from third to second place in each of those markets.

Summary and Conclusions

Concentration is a fact of economic life. However, con-

Table IV-3

Market Shares of Leading Companies, Selected Appliances, 1964, and 1966

A. Electric Knives

	1964	1966
Hamilton Beach	12%	28%
General Electric	42	24
Sunbeam	N.A.	12
Sears Roebuck	14	6

B. Blenders

	1964	1966
Oster (subsidiary of		
Sunbeam	27	28
Hamilton Beach	12	25
Waring	15	10
General Electric	N.A.	9
Sunbeam	N.A.	6

C. Food Mixers

	1964	1966
Sunbeam	43	40
Hamilton Beach	12	14
Dormeyer	15	12
General Electric	22	10
Sears Roebuck	N.A.	3

D. Portable Mixers

	1964	1966
Sunbeam	33	30
Hamilton Beach	15	27
General Electric	23	19
Dormeyer	8	5
Sears Roebuck	5	8

N.A. not available

Source: Advertising Age, August 29, 1966, p. 214.

centration ratios have limited significance as a measure of the intensity of competition. Some industries with high concentration are among the most competitive in our economy.

Concentration has not developed because of advertising. The main causes of economic concentration are found in technical forces which make feasible the economies of large-scale production and large-scale distribution, financial factors, and the development of national markets. It is important to keep cause and effect in proper perspective. Big business may lead to heavy advertising rather than heavy advertising creating big business.

There has been no relationship between the intensity of advertising and either the level of concentration or the trend of concentration (as measured by the Big Fours). The studies by Telser, Stigler, and the Federal Reserve Bank of Philadelphia all reached this conclusion. The analysis of Census data showed that in only 13 out of 50 industries did the Big Four in 1947 and 1958 consist of the same companies, but even within this group the relative rankings did not always remain unchanged. However, only one of these 13 industries had an advertising-sales ratio in excess of 3%. On the other hand, the 37 industries in which one or more of the 1947 Big Four had been replaced by 1958 included 12 with an advertising-sales ratio of more than 3%.

The data available for several industries show that the two leaders usually have been able to hold their top positions (they have sometimes changed ranks, as in cigarettes and beer). However, the other large companies in the market frequently have moved up or down in ranking. Moreover, for several industries (e.g., soft drinks and razor blades), although the same company retained first place during the period covered, its share of the market declined sharply.

The Big Fours have not been exclusive clubs. Their membership has changed—sometimes frequently—over relatively short periods of years. To retain membership, companies have had to be alert to new opportunities and to engage in extensive research and development in order to bring forth new and improved products. Even where a company has remained among the Big Four, its rank has often shifted with the tide of the consumer's favor and disfavor. Despite the power of the purse and barriers to entry, new entrants to the market have successfully breached the citadel and replaced the alleged holders of market power among the industry leaders. The top as reflected in the Big Four has proved to be slippery in all but a few markets.

Large-scale advertising is more a manifestation of intense competition than a cause of monopoly or oligopoly.[65] For many products, it has been accompanied by an expanding volume of industry sales and by dramatic changes in market shares rather than by an increase in economic concentration.

Mr. Kaldor, a severe critic of advertising, has stated that if advertising did not promote economic concentration, "the whole discussion about the effects of advertising on the efficiency of the economic system would be irrelevant." The statistical data here reviewed indicate that the extent of concentration among the largest companies in an industry has not been determined by the intensity of advertising. By Mr. Kaldor's test, therefore, the discussion is "irrelevant."

65 Professor Telser concluded that the characteristics of heavily advertised products " . . . show why oligopolies producing certain kinds of products might advertise intensively. It does not imply the converse that advertising can explain the competitive structure of the industry." Lester G. Telser, "How Much Does It Pay Whom to Advertise?" *American Economic Review, Papers and Proceedings,* December 1960, p. 202.

In a study of British experience, P.K. Else noted that "in oligopolistic trades advertising is likely to be subject to some sort of ratchet effect . . . The advertising-sales ratio . . . would tend to be higher in such an oligopolistic trade than in a trade with a large number of firms but which is otherwise similar in terms of the level of manufacturers' sales and the number of products . . . The effect of one firm's actions on others is likely to be much greater when the others are few in number than when it is spread over a large number." Mr. Else concluded that in England for " . . . Soap and Detergents, Toothpaste and Powders, and Health Drinks, the size of the advertising-sales ratio is considerably influenced by the forces of oligopolistic competition." P. K. Else, "The Incidence of Advertising in Manufacturing Industries," *Oxford Economic Papers,* March 1966, pp. 98-100, 105.

V

Advertising and Prices

Intensive advertising is alleged to raise prices for one of two reasons: 1] advertising helps create a monopoly position for brand items thus insulating them from price competition and 2] the high cost of advertising adds to total costs which prices must be high enough to cover.

Advertising and Monopoly Prices

According to Donald F. Turner "heavy advertising outlays lead . . . to the establishment of high monopolistic prices."[1] To support this conclusion he stated that consumer goods industries "with high advertising outlays tended to earn profit rates which were about 50% higher than those which did not undertake a significant effort."[2] In the next chapter, the relationship between advertising outlays and profits will be examined.

A company does not set prices in a vacuum. Even if it is able to pre-empt part of the market because of product

1 Turner, *op. cit.,* p. 2. Professor Bach holds that "Increased product differentiation lets each firm boost its price somewhat." Bach, *op. cit.,* p. 439.

2 Turner, *op. cit.,* p. 3.

differentiation, the availability of competitive and substitute products cannot be ignored. If it brings out a product which is already on the market, it must set the price at a level which is competitive within the existing structure of prices. A company has greater freedom of action in connection with a completely new product—a much rarer situation—but even here it cannot ignore possible alternatives and potential competition.

Sandage and Fryburger have pointed out:

> The volume of advertising may be a potent factor in influencing human attitudes or building up public preference for a particular brand. *Such a monopoly, however, will provide only slight power to increase prices.* Any attempt to raise prices an appreciable degree will encourage smaller companies to come in the market with a lower-priced product. There is also the ever-present element of consumer shifts of choice to other products.
>
> . . . Some manufacturers in new industries have been able to build up a near monopoly in the minds of consumers for a short period of time, but not a monopoly of supply. Such names as Frigidaire, Victrola, and Kodak were, at one time, almost generic names and as such, might be considered to have certain of the attributes of a monopoly. Competitors, however, were able to break this hold on consumer attitudes through their own use of advertising.[3] (Italics added)

Similarly, Professor Telser has concluded that although advertised goods usually sell at a premium as compared with nonadvertised goods, "This finding . . . does not permit the conclusion that advertising is a source of monopoly profit." He attributes the difference to "higher average quality," less variation in quality, and the information provided by advertising.[4]

The price behavior of brand-name products, whether heavily advertised or not, differs from that of standardized products such as wheat. Prices for brands tend to be more

3 Sandage and Fryburger, *op. cit.,* pp. 49-50.
4 Telser, "Advertising and Competition," *op. cit.,* p. 542.

rigid, neither advancing as much nor declining as much as those for other products, with price changes tending to lag behind those in other industries.

Much of the charge concerning monopoly prices is related to the insulation of these prices from immediate response to changes in supply or demand. That the prices of branded items are not always completely rigid is illustrated by the price specials periodically offered for some products such as detergents and dry groceries. Moreover, as Neil Borden has noted, when demand declines, "price competition was found to come into play sooner or later."[5]

Sometimes, this price competition develops through private brands or by the development of new brands, as was noted in Chapter III. Nevertheless, prices of brand-name products tend to be more rigid. Nonprice competition (e.g., improved products, advertising and other promotion, quality changes, etc.), rather than price competition, characterizes these products—as is true for most goods and services whether heavily advertised or not.

Advertising Costs and Prices

A company must recover all of its costs, including those for advertising, if it is to be profitable or to survive over the long run. Does this mean that relatively large advertising costs will tend to increase prices as some have contended?[6] The argument that high costs of advertising lead to higher prices may be summarized as follows:

1] Advertising encourages product differentiation in order to develop selling points.

2] The differentiated product then pre-empts a share of the market by building up customer loyalty.

5 Borden, *op. cit.,* p. 850.

6 Kaldor, *op. cit.,* p. 10. The British Monopolies Commission concluded that for detergents: "Our view is that competition between Unilever and P & G tends to result in the escalation of advertising and promotion costs and to that extent to increase the price that the public is required to pay." "Household Detergents," *op. cit.,* p. 41.

3] This makes demand less elastic, that is, less responsive to changes in price.

4] As a result, the firm is able to charge higher prices.

This is an oversimplified and incomplete portrayal of the realities of the market. It does not give sufficient emphasis to the competitive pressures which are constantly eroding market shares of differentiated products as described in Chapter III, and it ignores the changing volume-cost-price relationships which develop when the product succeeds in attracting an enlarged demand. The situation must be viewed as dynamic, not static.

If volume does increase substantially—that is, if the advertising is successful—then it often is possible to effect economies of scale and thus to reduce the unit costs of production and of overhead.[7] If the net effect is a lower price, it is still possible to increase profits because of the greater volume.

Robert V. Zacher has pointed out:

> Many items are being manufactured today, on a mass production basis, at costs which are below those which applied many years ago when prices of labor and material were far less. This has been accomplished through the efficiencies of mass production. This in turn is an outgrowth of mass consumption made possible through widespread advertising effort.[8]

Unit costs of production can also be favorably affected by operations close to capacity. Charles Mortimer, then chairman of the board of General Foods, has described how advertising paid off for that company in terms of its impact on sales volume and the resulting rate of operations.

> It pays by developing such a large and dependable volume of sales that:

---

7 For example, Procter and Gamble has reported: "But as demonstrated time and again in our Company, effective advertising brings about savings—in the costs of manufacturing, distribution, buying, and other operations—that clearly result in lower prices to the consumer." *Annual Report, For Year Ended June 30, 1966,* p. 8.

8 Robert V. Zacher, *Advertising Techniques and Management,* Richard D. Irwin, Homewood, Illinois, 1961, p. 584.

1] We can keep our plants running at high efficiency in terms of processes and machine operations. And I hardly need remind you of the importance of this, steadily increasing costs being what they are.

2] We can utilize the special skills and the time and energy of our people to full advantage.

3] We can turn our inventories and raw materials rapidly, and hence keep our working capital turning swiftly and profitably.[9]

Mass production requires mass markets which can more readily be developed (pre-sold) for many products through advertising than by other means of sales promotion.[10] To the extent that unit production costs decline, the amount spent for advertising may be offset in whole or in part by such production economies. In other words, total unit costs may actually be lower as a result of large-scale advertising than in its absence. Under these conditions, advertising costs could become a larger percentage of the lower total unit costs.

The reverse may also be true, as for example, where product innovation takes place frequently and shortens the life cycle of the older products. Under these conditions, total unit costs would tend to rise. Actually, the life cycle of a new product probably involves declining unit costs during the phase of expanding demand, some stability in costs when peak volume is achieved, and then rising unit costs as volume declines. In the latter period, it would be impossible to raise prices without accelerating the decline in demand.

It is clearly erroneous to assume that the proportion shown for advertising always involves a *net* increase in total

9 Cited in Sandage and Fryburger, *op. cit.,* pp. 40-41.

10 However, the Reith Report (p. 40) states that " . . . advertising cannot be justified on the grounds that the concentration it helps bring about and sustain produces economies of mass scale production. For to the extent that concentration is justified by such economies, price competition would have had the same effect in a way more beneficial to the consumer." This is a questionable conclusion for two reasons: there is no assurance that the price cut would stimulate volume as much as advertising and an increase in volume does not necessarily mean an increase in concentration.

costs; it may reflect some increase or it may result in an actual decline in unit costs or it may be "indeterminate."[11] Moreover, if the money were not spent for advertising, it is probable that expenditures would have to be made for other means of selling and/or promotion so that in this sense, too, the total cost of advertising cannot be considered a net increase in total costs.

Wroe Alderson concluded "The economic justification of advertising rests on the assumption that advertising offers a shorter route to market than could be found in any other way." He reported: "The president of the Lambert Pharmacal Company, makers of Listerine, was once asked why his company spent so much for advertising. 'It is very simple,' he replied. 'It would cost me more to sell my product by any other means.'"[12] To the extent that this same conclusion applies to other products, the replacement of advertising by other means of promotion would add to total costs.

Factors Determining Prices

Even more important than the qualifications noted above is the fundamental misconception of the role of costs in price determination implicit in the assumption that large advertising costs directly determine price. There are many factors which a company official must consider and evaluate when he establishes a price. These include the economic characteristics of product,[13] competition, demand, costs, distribution system used, legal factors, political factors, and public relations. The combination of these factors which may be significant varies for different products produced by a com-

---

11 For a discussion of the relationship between advertising costs and production costs see Borden, *op. cit.,* pp. 854-57. He stated " . . . it is impossible from cost data to trace a clear causal relationship between decreased production costs and advertising."

12 Alderson, *op. cit.,* pp. 134-35.

13 For a more complete discussion, see Jules Backman, *Pricing: Policies and Practices,* National Industrial Conference Board, New York, 1961.

pany and for the same product over a period of time. Freedom of action in setting prices is limited by the operation of these forces. There is no way in which they can be fed into a computer to determine the "right" price. It is the informed judgment of the price maker which fuses these several factors into a final decision concerning price. Pricing is an art, not a science.

It will be noted that cost is only *one* factor considered in pricing and that advertising costs are only part of total costs. Even so, it is extremely difficult for a multiproduct company to determine costs accurately for many products for a variety of reasons. For such companies, cost accounting by product and detailed cost allocation often tend to be extremely difficult and hence must be arbitrary. For example, research laboratories work on numerous projects simultaneously and in addition must make allowance for failures as well successes. As a result it is almost impossible to assign all research costs to specific products.

Costs determine profitability, rather than price. Competition usually is of primary importance in price determination. When prices do not yield satisfactory profits at the prevailing level of costs, a company must either reduce its cost, seek to expand volume, or withdraw from producing the affected product. It cannot merely add to its costs, however determined, some desired profit margin and expect that consumers will pay that price. This is especially true during periods of business decline.

The pricing of new products is important because such a large proportion of the sales volume in recent years has been derived from such products. New products fall into two categories: 1] those which are minor modifications of, identical with, or equivalent to existing products and 2] those which are entirely new products. In pricing new products, a company has much less freedom of action for products in the first group than for those in the second group.

The fact that an equivalent product is available to meet the specific need means that the new product must be slotted into the existing price structure, with due allowance for differences in quality. In other words, the product may be a new addition to the producing company's line but not to the market. The primary factor considered in pricing such a "new" product is the price of competing or substitute products. Costs can play a role in the decision as to whether the company should manufacture the product because, in relationship to the prevailing price structure, they indicate whether the venture can or will be profitable; however, costs neither determine nor influence the price.

For products which are genuinely new, several factors must be considered: (1) the prices of equivalent products produced by other industries; (2) the magnitude of the investment in research and development costs and the philosophy concerning how this investment should be recovered; (3) estimates of demand and its elasticity; and (4) alternative estimates of production and selling costs.

In connection with new products, costs are so closely related to volume and to decisions concerning the allocation of research costs and starting-up expenses that a wide range of cost figures can be obtained. For new products, the company's philosophy of pricing may be the primary determinant of the initial offering price. Should a price be set high initially and then reduced as experience with consumer acceptability, production techniques, and costs is accumulated? Or should a much lower price be set initially to tap a mass market from the outset? In either case, costs play a minor role. Thus, it is evident that a single type of costs, such as advertising, usually has practically no impact on price determination.[14]

Professor John M. Clark has concluded that any evaluation of the impact of advertising on total costs cannot

14 Alfred A. Kuehn has noted that " . . . *advertising costs are not transmitted directly to price!"* (His Italics.) "Important Factors In Effective Advertising Expenditures" in *Effective Marketing Coordination,* George L. Baker, Jr., editor, Proceedings of the Forty-Fourth National Conference of the American Marketing Association, Los Angeles, Cal., 1961, p. 346.

be limited to the arithmetic of specific costs:

> One further question which must not be ignored is whether advertising, while tending to keep production cost down by maintaining an efficiently large scale of production, may increase total cost by the addition of the cost of the advertising itself. To this question no simple and certain answer can be given. But there is a strong case for the conclusion that, *if there is such an increase in total cost, it is outweighed by the residuum of net gain resulting from the dynamics of new-product development, which is necessary to a rising standard of living plus the progress in productive efficiency made possible by the large-scale production, which in turn is made possible by advertising.*[15] (Italics added.)

Finally, advertising may influence the price by building up consumer acceptance of a product at a designated price. In this way, advertising affects the price through the demand side rather than through costs.

Price Appeal v. Heavy Advertising

It is sometimes suggested that instead of heavy advertising, prices should be reduced and thus benefit the consumer directly.[16] The desirability of such a policy depends upon the impact on demand of each alternative.[17] The relative results obtained from 5% of sales spent for advertising, for example, must be measured against the increase in volume achieved by a reduction in price. In the first place, this percentage refers to the manufacturer's price and not to the retail price. If the retailer uses a *fixed percentage markup,* a given percentage reduction in the manufacturer's price will be translated into the same percentage cut in retail prices. However, if the retailer does not pass on all of these savings, the reduction in retail price will be smaller than in

15 Clark, *op. cit.,* pp. 264-65.
16 The British Monopolies Commission recommended large reductions in selling expenses, including advertising, and in prices for detergents. "Household Detergents," *op. cit.,* pp. 41-42, 44-45.
17 If the expenditures for advertising lead to a rise in unit costs and, in turn, in prices as is often stated, then this factor would have to enter the calculation.

the wholesale price. Historically, retail prices have fluctuated less than wholesale prices.[18] It is probable, therefore, that the maxium percentage reduction to be anticipated in the retail price would be less than that in the manufacturer's price.

Unless the elasticity of demand[19] is so great that a price cut can yield the same or a greater increase in volume than comparable expenditures on advertising, it would not be advantageous to a firm to elect the price cut.[20] For example, Robert Headen and James W. McKie have concluded "It is extremely doubtful if an across-the board, industrywide price cut of 10 to 20 percent would increase the total amount of cereals consumed."[21] Under such conditions, there is a much greater incentive to concentrate a firm's efforts on advertising and other forms of promotion.

Moreover, as was noted earlier, the large volume generated by advertising can lead to reductions in unit costs of production which can offset in whole or in part the unit cost of advertising.[22] If a price cut fails to result in an equally large increase in volume, the economies in production costs may not be fully realized and a company may find itself operating at a lower profit or in the red. If the economies are large enough, the consumer may in time pay a lower price as a result of the demand stimulated by advertising and other promotional efforts than the initial lower price adopted as an alternative to such selling activities.

18 An exception is found during the 1957-59 to 1964 period. See "Inflation and the Price Indexes." *op. cit.,* pp. 59-60, 123-27.

19 The percentage increase in demand that will accompany each 1% cut in price. Professor E. H. Chamberlin has suggested that "By spreading ... knowledge, advertising makes the demand for [a] product more elastic." Chamberlin, *op. cit.,* p. 118.

20 Where the results of a price cut and an expenditure for advertising are the same, the consumer would undoubtedly prefer the price cut.

21 Cited in "Grocery Manufacturing," *op. cit.,* p. 169.

22 It has been pointed out that: "A price reduction is a once-for-all operation, whereas an advertising expenditure costing a sum equivalent to the loss of income through the price reduction may keep the product's name before the public for months or years." Taplin, *op. cit.,* p. 109.

A distinction must also be made between the impact of a price cut on the total demand for a product and the results experienced by a single company in the market. If a company could establish a price differential in its favor as compared with completely substitutable products, it could expand its own sales substantially at the expense of its competitors. But the probability that its competitors would be willing to suffer the loss in volume or in market shares without meeting the price cut is virtually nil. Thus, in the absence of evidence that a price reduction will expand the total demand for the industry's products and that a company would get a share of this enlarged demand, a firm would be loath to attempt to stimulate demand in that manner.

For many products, the consumer already has a choice between well-known brands and private or lesser-known brands at lower prices.[23] Otto Kleppner has observed: "Products that are not advertised enjoy benefits that accrue to an industry as a whole by virtue of those products in the industry that are advertised . . . there is no basis for believing that the unadvertised brands would be as cheaply sold or as widely available if there were no brands available."[24] This is a significant observation which too often is ignored. Advertising

23 A study of the prices of private and manufacturers' brands in the 1960-63 period for three grocery products concluded: ". . . price is the primary appeal for the private label retailer brands of bread, frozen orange concentrate and margarine. A 5 cent discount on a 23 cent loaf of bread, a 5½ cent discount on a 30 cent can of orange concentrate and a 10 cent discount on a 29 cent pound of margarine indicate the magnitude of these price discounts." Ray A. Goldberg, *The Dynamics of Brand Competition,* An Address before the Grocery Manufacturers of America, Inc., White Sulphur Springs, West Virginia, June 14, 15, 16, 1965 (mimeo), p. 19. A study by Daniel M. Slate and Robert V. Mitchell, of the University of Illinois, of 19 manufacturers, who produce private brands, showed that they sold them "at a price lower than the price received for the manufacturer's advertised brand . . . " Daniel M. Slate and Robert V. Mitchell, *Brand Competition In the Food Processing Industry,* Arthur D. Little, Inc., Report to the National Commission on Food Marketing for the Grocery Manufacturers of America, Inc., January 1966, p. 116.

24 Otto Kleppner, *Advertising Procedure,* Fourth Edition, Prentice-Hall, Inc., Englewood Cliffs, N. J., January 1956, pp. 676-77.

not only makes the consumer aware of the advertised brand but of that line of products as well. Thus, for example, an advertiser of toothpaste educates the consumer about the advantages of using dentifrices and this benefits all sellers of that product, not the advertiser alone.

The consumer often prefers the higher-priced, well-known brand although there has been a growth of private brands, particularly for foods, as is noted elsewhere. Thus, if the money spent for advertising were largely used for price cuts with the accompanying anonymity of the brand, consumers would obtain less information about the product, and the result might very well be a reduction in demand and an accompanying paring of or disappearance of profits. As a result, price reductions are not always meaningful alternatives to advertising, particularly for top-line quality items.[25]

Moreover, the higher price for advertised brands reflects in part the uniformity of their quality and the premium the consumer is willing to pay because it is produced by a company in which they have confidence. As Professor George J. Stigler has pointed out:

> "Reputation" is a word which denotes the persistence of quality and reputation commands a price (or exacts a penalty) because it economizes on search. When economists deplore the reliance of the consumer on reputation . . . they implicitly assume that the consumer has a large laboratory, ready to deliver current information quickly and gratuitously.[26]

Thus, there is a sound economic reason for an advertised brand to command a price premium as compared with one which is not advertised. The latter product, in effect, represents an offering of a different bundle of goods and services than the advertised brand.

25 The National Commission on Food Marketing concluded: "One-stop shopping by consumers reduces their sensitivity to prices of individual foods (unless featured), and weakens the pressure on retailers to keep every retail price aligned with the corresponding wholesale price. Higher incomes make consumers less willing to vary purchases in response to moderate price changes." "Food From Farmer To Consumer," *op. cit.,* p. 98.
26 "The Economics of Information," *op. cit.,* p. 224.

An increase in advertising expenditures is the more attractive alternative to a firm because 1] competitors may fail to match them or could do so only after some period of time,[27] or 2] a firm may believe it could mount a more effective advertising campaign than its competitors. If a large unsatisfied demand is available, both the company and its competitors may benefit from making consumers more fully aware of the usefulness and merits of the product.

Walter Taplin has pointed out that "price reduction and advertising expenditure are not necessarily alternatives. They are both tools of marketing, but it is wrong to assume that the job which they do is the same in each case. This is particularly clear when we draw a distinction between established products and those newly introduced."[28]

For products which are entirely new, a carefully balanced combination of price reductions over time as the product becomes more widely accepted plus heavy advertising may yield the best results. This is particularly true for big ticket items as the postwar experience first with black and white television and more recently with color television has demonstrated. However, many of the most heavily advertised products sell for less than a dollar, so that the impact of price changes may not be so great as for big-ticket items. It may be questioned whether price cuts of, say, 5% to 10% would stimulate significantly the demand for many products which sell for less than a dollar.

Although the issue has been posed in terms of either/or, in actual practice some combination of both policies often takes place.[29] There are many businessmen who believe that advertising tends to lower prices. In a *Harvard Business*

27 Joel Dean has pointed out "Rivals reactions to advertising are less certain, less immediate, and less precisely imitative than are their price reactions." Dean, *op. cit.,* p. 354.

28 Taplin, *op. cit.,* p. 123.

29 "Even firms that rely primarily on the appeal of low prices must do some advertising; if they did not, their low price offering might not be noticed by many customers." Alfred R. Oxenfeldt, *Pricing For Marketing Executives,* Wadsworth Publishing Company, Inc., San Francisco, Cal., 1961, p. 10.

Review survey, businessmen were asked about the relationship between advertising and prices both affirmatively and
negatively. Their responses are shown below:[30]

	Advertising's Effect On Prices	
	Lower Prices	**Higher Prices**
	(percent)	
Generally Agree	30	14
Partially Agree	24	14
	54	28
Can't say	13	10
Partially Disagree	14	17
Generally Disagree	19	45
	33	62
Total	100	100

On the basis of these data, it was concluded that "Advertising's effect is in the *direction of lower prices.* Over half
the respondents answer this way regardless of question form.
However, a substantial minority disagree."[31] (Italics added.)

Relative Importance of Advertising by Industries

Advertising plays widely varying roles in the marketing
strategy of different industries. In broad terms these variations
are portrayed in the data compiled by the Internal Revenue
Service from corporate income-tax returns. Appendix Table
E-6 shows the percentage of total compiled receipts spent
for advertising for 68 major industries and industry subgroups
for corporate tax years ending between July 1962 and June
1963; these data cover mainly the calendar year 1962. These
data—the latest available in 1966—are several years old,
but they serve to show the general relationships prevailing
among industries.

These data are subject to several limitations. First, they
represent broad industry composites rather than the experience with individual products or companies. Within an industry the intensity of advertising usually varies widely among
products. The composite figure for the industry conceals

30 Greyser, *op. cit.,* p. 28.   31 *Ibid.*

these variations, and hence the data do not show the extent to which some companies emphasize advertising.

Second, the Internal Revenue Service requests companies to classify themselves within the Standard Industrial Classification on the basis of their preponderant product. This means that the totals include a considerable volume of sales for secondary or unrelated products for which the advertising strategy may vary markedly from that for the primary products. Moreover, companies within an industry classification usually have varying proportions of their sales in these secondary lines which can and do differ among companies.

Third, contribution to a final product may be made by several industries and yet each industry reports only its own advertising cost. The cumulative advertising cost for some products may, therefore, be higher than indicated by these industry data.

Fourth, companies define advertising in different ways.[32]

These limitations indicate that the relationships reported cannot be used as exact yardsticks for specific products or industries. Yet these data may be helpful to show the broad range of experience in American industry.

In 1962, American corporations reported they spent $10,391 million on advertising or 1.09% of their total compiled receipts. In other words, slightly more than $1 was spent for every $100 of sales; for retail stores the total was $1.51, and for manufacturing it was $1.38. In several major industries the proportions fell far short of these totals. For example, metal mining spent only 2 cents per $100 of sales, construction 24 cents, and electric and gas 30 cents.

At the other extreme, the tobacco industry spent $5.25, beverages $4.91, motion pictures $3.19, chemicals and allied

32 It has been suggested that "Individual companies determine for themselves the kind of expenditures they wish to classify as advertising for tax purposes. In most instances, therefore, they undoubtedly include expenses other than those incurred for the purchase of time and space, or in the preparation of promotional material." *Advertising Age,* July 6, 1964, p. 59.

products $3.88,[33] and food and kindred products $2.01. (See Chart V-1.) At the retail level, expenditures for advertising

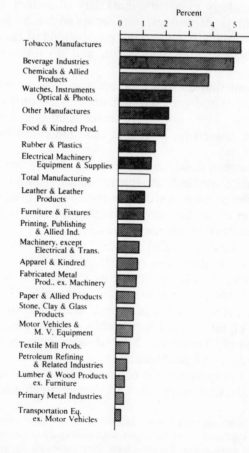

CHART V-1

Advertising as a Percent of Compiled Receipts by Manufacturing Industries, July 1962-June 1963

Percent

Tobacco Manufactures	
Beverage Industries	
Chemicals & Allied Products	
Watches, Instruments Optical & Photo.	
Other Manufactures	
Food & Kindred Prod.	
Rubber & Plastics	
Electrical Machinery Equipment & Supplies	
Total Manufacturing	
Leather & Leather Products	
Furniture & Fixtures	
Printing, Publishing & Allied Ind.	
Machinery, except Electrical & Trans.	
Apparel & Kindred	
Fabricated Metal Prod., ex. Machinery	
Paper & Allied Products	
Stone, Clay & Glass Products	
Motor Vehicles & M. V. Equipment	
Textile Mill Prods.	
Petroleum Refining & Related Industries	
Lumber & Wood Products ex. Furniture	
Primary Metal Industries	
Transportation Eq. ex. Motor Vehicles	

33 This category includes drugs and toilet preparations which have among the highest ratios of advertising expense to sales. The industry

ranged from 85 cents per $100 of sales for automotive dealers and gasoline service stations, which are backed up by manufacturer's advertising, to $2.90 for furniture and home furnishings and equipment stores; for food stores the ratio was $1.31. (See Chart V-2.) Advertising is used most widely by consumer goods industries in the manufacturing sector of the economy, by retail trade, and in the personal service industries. Producers of industrial products, mining, and public utilities place relatively little emphasis upon advertising.

The ratio of 1.09% for all corporations does not show the net impact on the price paid by the final consumer. Total compiled receipts reflect successive stages of production as

CHART V-2
Advertising as a Percent of Compiled Receipts by Retail Trade, July 1962-June 1963

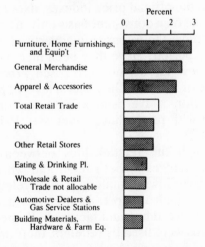

average is reduced substantially because about half the sales are industrial chemicals for which relatively small amounts are spent on advertising. This industry provides a good illustration of one limitation inherent in using composite data.

well as wholesale and retail trade. One indication of the extent of the duplication is found in the fact that total compiled receipts for corporations alone aggregated $949 billion in 1962 as compared with a gross corporate national product of $317 billion.

As was noted earlier, a more accurate picture of the impact of advertising on the final consumer is shown by the ratio to personal consumption expenditures; this averaged 3.49% in 1962 and 3.54% in 1965.[34]

Advertising and Price Inflation

During the past quarter of a century, our economy has experienced considerable price inflation. This inflation has largely reflected the fiscal and monetary pressures arising out of World War II, the Korean War, and Vietnam, and to some extent the accompanying labor cost inflation. Prices of various products and groups of products have responded differently to these underlying pressures. Because of periodic changes in the official price indexes, data for many products are available on a consistent basis only after 1947.

How have the intensively advertised products behaved during this period? Have they been increased more than the prices of less intensively advertised products? Have they risen more or less than the general level of prices? To answer these questions, advertising-sales ratios for 1962 have been compared with price changes between 1947 and 1966. (See Appendix C)

Although the relationships between advertising-sales ratios and changes in both retail and wholesale prices are shown in the following analysis, it is the relationship to wholesale prices which is most significant, since they represent the prices charged by manufacturers. If unchanging percentage markups were used by retailers, there would be identical

---

34 Based on the *Printers' Ink* tabulations, which in 1962 reported the total cost of advertising as $12,381 million or $1,990 million greater than reported by the Internal Revenue Service.

increases for both retail and wholesale prices. However, retail markups change and usually are not controlled by the manufacturer. Moreover, the advertising ratios reflect only the experience of the manufacturers. Retailers also spend considerable sums for advertising, and their pattern of expenditures varies from that of the manufacturers.[35] Thus, the relationships of advertising to retail prices are less meaningful than those to wholesale prices. However, since there is considerable interest in retail prices, both types of relationship have been examined.

WHOLESALE PRICE CHANGES

1947 to 1965: Appendix Table C-1 shows the relationship between the advertising-sales ratio in 1962 and the magnitude of the changes for 29 groups of wholesale prices between 1947 and 1965. These data are summarized below:

Advertising-Sales Ratio (percent)	Wholesale Price Changes, 1947 to 1965		
	Decline	Below Average Increase	Above Average Increase
14-15		1	
12-13		1	
9-10	1		
6-7			1
5-6		1	1
4-5	1	1	
3-4		1	2
2-3	2	1	2
1-2	2		5
0-1		4	2
	6	10	13

Between 1947 and 1965, the comprehensive wholesale price index increased 26.2%. Of six industries with an

35 For example, the Internal Revenue Service data for 1962 show that drugstores spend 1.37% of their sales for advertising or less than the average of 1.51% for all retail stores. In contrast, as is shown in Appendix Table C-1, drug manufacturers have among the highest advertising ratios. These data were reported in *Advertising Age,* June 7, 1965, p. 102.

advertising-sales ratio above 5%, one reported a decline in prices, (drugs), three below-average increases, (toilet preparations, soaps and detergents, and clocks and watches), and two (tobacco and beer and malt)[36] above-average increases. Of five industries with advertising-sales ratios between 3% and 5%, two had above-average price increases. Thus, seven industries with an advertising-sales ratio of 3% or more reported price declines or less than average increases while only four had above-average increases in prices.

For thirteen industries with an advertising-sales ratio of less than 2%, seven recorded larger than average increases in prices while six had below-average increases or decreases.

The relationship between the advertising-sales ratio and the changes in wholesale prices has been computed. (See Appendix C) Chart V-3 shows the data. Each dot represents one industry (identified in Appendix Table C-1) and shows the level of the advertising-sales ratio and the change in prices for the period covered. The line of relationship would rise sharply from left to right if any general relationship prevailed. But the line of relationship shown on Chart V-3 moves downward, not upward, thus suggesting that the greater the intensity of advertising, the smaller the price rise during the postwar price inflation. However, the dots are so widely scattered that it is clear the varying intensities of advertising have little or no impact on the changes in prices.[37]

1957-59 to June 1966: Shorter-term relationships are shown on Chart C-1 (Appendix C) which covers the period 1957-59 to June 1966. Statistical analysis reveals no relationship between the level of advertising expenditures and changes in wholesale prices for the period since 1957-59.[38] In 14 of the 30 industries for which data are available prices rose

36 The BLS indexes for wholesale prices exclude taxes.
37 The coefficient of correlation (r) was −.0943 and the coefficient of determination (r²) was .0089.
38 The coefficient of correlation was .0123 and the coefficient of determination was .0002.

more and in 6 prices rose less than the 5.7% increase in
the WPI in this period; prices declined for 10 groups. (Derived from Appendix C-1)

CHART V-3
Advertising Outlays per Dollar of Sales,
1962, and Percent Change in Wholesale Prices
For Selected Commodities, 1947 to 1965

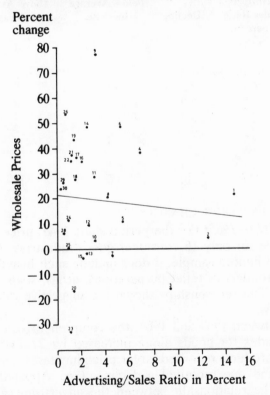

Of the six industries with an advertising-sales ratio
above 5%, two recorded price declines, two a smaller increase
than the WPI, and two larger increases. At the other extreme,
the fourteen industries with advertising-sales ratios of less

than two percent recorded four decreases and three less than average increases; seven had above-average increases.

On the basis of this record, during the postwar price inflation companies which engaged in intensive advertising generally have not been raising their prices more rapidly than those with relatively smaller advertising outlays.

Wholesale Price Changes, 1957-59 to June 1966

Advertising–Sales Ratio (percent)	Decline	Below Average Increase	Above Average Increase
14-15			1
12-13		1	
9-10	1		
6-7		1	
5-6	1		1
4-5	1		1
3-4			3
2-3	3	1	1
1-2	3		4
0-1	1	3	3
Total	10	6	14

RETAIL PRICE CHANGES

1947 to 1965: For the period since 1947, price data are available for only 16 consumer goods industries. Although this is a limited sample, it does include such heavily advertised products as toilet preparations, drugs, soaps, and tobacco. The relationships shown are suggestive rather than definitive.

Between 1947 and 1965, the comprehensive consumer price index for goods alone increased by 27.6%;[39] five of the 16 products recorded larger price increases, ten smaller ones, and one recorded a decline. (See Appendix Table C-2.) The relationship between the advertising-sales ratio and the magnitude of the retail price rise in the 18-year period is shown on the next page.

---

[39] The comprehensive consumer price index for goods *and* services increased 41.3% between 1947 and 1965.

Advertising-Sales Ratio (per cent)	Retail Price Changes, 1947 to 1965		
	Decline	Below Average Increase	Above Average Increase
14-15		1	
12-13		1	
9-10		1	
5-6			1
3-4		1	
2-3	1	1	1
1-2		2	1
0-1		3	2
	1	10	5

The three industries with the highest advertising ratio had less than average price rises (drugs 22.5%, toilet preparations 15.9%, soaps 1.2%). Two of the five industries with above-average price rises had advertising ratios of less than one percent (motor vehicles 45.8%, meats 31.8%). These data show a tendency for the most intensive users of advertising to have had somewhat smaller increases in retail prices during the postwar period.[40] (See Chart C-2.)

1957-59 to June 1966: There was also little statistical relationship between the level of the advertising-sales ratio and the changes in retail prices between 1957-59 and June 1966.[41] (See Chart C-3.)

For this shorter period, data were available for 22 groups of consumer goods industries. Thirteen groups of prices rose less than 9.0%,[42] the increase in the consumer price index for goods, while 9 rose more. (See Appendix Table C-2.)

The relationship between the advertising-sales ratio and the magnitude of price changes may be summarized as follows:

For five industries with an advertising-sales ratio of above 5%, one recorded an above-average price increase,

40 The coefficient of correlation was .1464 and the coefficient of determination was .0214.

41 The coefficient of correlation was -.0970 and the coefficient of determination was .0094.

42 The consumer price index for goods *and* services increased by 12.9% in this period.

Advertising-Sales Ratio (per cent)	Retail Price Changes, 1957-59 to June 1966		
	Decline	Below Average Increase	Above Average Increase
14-15		1	
12-13		1	
9-10	1		
6-7		1	
5-6			1
4-5	1		
3-4			1
2-3	1	2	2
1-2	1	2	2
0-1	$\frac{1}{5}$	$\frac{1}{8}$	$\frac{3}{9}$

three below-average increases, and one a decline. Of the 5 industries with an advertising-sales ratio of less than 1%, three had above-average increases in prices. Again, the most intensive advertisers tended to have the smallest price increases.

FOOD PRICES

The National Commission on Food Marketing has reported estimates of the cost of advertising *and* other promotion costs for 21 food products in 1964. (See Appendix Table E-7). The promotion costs include a mixture of price competition and non-price competition, but there is no indication as to the relative costs of each.[43] For five products, salesmen's salaries and brokerage also were included in the total for promotion, but there is no indication of their relative importance. Thus, the Commission's data show ratios which are greater than for advertising alone. For the broader categories of food products covered, the IRS data (See Appendix Table C-1) show a range of advertising-sales ratios between 0.28% for sugar and 3.18% for grain-mill products.

Because of the seasonal nature of supplies of several of the food products listed, seasonal price movements are significant. Comparisons based on full years tend to avoid

43 "Food From Farmer to Consumer," *op. cit.,* pp. 63-64.

seasonal distortions which might be reflected in monthly data.

The Commission concluded that "When a few large firms dominate a field, they frequently forbear from competing actively by price; competition by advertising, sales promotion, and other selling efforts almost always increases; and the market power inescapably at the disposal of such firms may be used to impose onerous terms upon suppliers or customers."[44] To support this broad generalization, the Commission reported that cereal prices had risen much more than the BLS retail food price index between 1954 and 1964.

One illustration is not a sound basis for such a broad conclusion. By careful selection of illustrations the opposite conclusion also can be drawn. For example, between 1957-59 and 1965, both evaporated milk and processed fruits and vegetables with promotion costs of 6% had smaller increases in prices (5.3% and 7.3% respectively) than the rise of 8.8% in the BLS retail food price index. A meaningful conclusion must be based upon examination of *all* the evidence.

1947-1965: For the period, 1947 to 1965, *retail* price data were available for 17 of the 21 food products. During that period, the food component of the CPI rose 33.8%. Prices of seven products in the group rose more than the average and ten rose less than the average or declined. (See Appendix Table E-7.)

For four of the seven foods with *above-average* increases in prices, sales promotion accounted for less than 3% of total sales.

Of the ten foods with *below-average* increases or declines in prices none had a sales promotion ratio of less than 3% while three had ratios above 4%.

For eight foods with a sales promotion ratio between 3% and 3.5%, the changes in prices ranged between a decline of 28.3% for broilers and an increase of 84.7% for Florida oranges.

For five foods with a sales promotion ratio above

44 *Ibid.,* p. 94.

4%, the range of price increases was between nothing for canned tomatoes and 100.8% for cornflakes.

Clearly, there was a little relationship between the relative magnitude of sales promotion and the retail price changes recorded for these selected food products during the postwar period.

For the eight *wholesale* food products with above-average price increases, three had promotion to sales ratios above 4% and five had ratios between 3% and 3-½%. The ten wholesale prices with less than average increases including two declines were divided: three products with promotion to sales ratios above 4%, four with 3% to 3-½% ratios, and three with ratios below 3%. Clearly, the pattern for wholesale prices was similar to that for retail prices.

1957-59 to 1965: The tabulation below summarizes the relationship between promotion as a percent of sales and changes in 18 *retail* food prices between 1957-59 to 1965.[45]

That there has been no relationship between the magnitude of retail price inflation and the relative promotion costs for food products is clear. This is most evident from the diverse behavior for the eight products for which promotion costs averaged between 3 and 3.5%. Within this group, retail prices were lower in 1965 than in the 1957-59 base period for two products (broilers, −9.7% and eggs, −7.2%), increased less than the average (8.8%) for two prod-

	Changes In Retail Prices, 1957-59 to 1965		
Promotion as		Below Average	Above Average
% of Sales	Decline	Increase	Increase
20			1
6-7		2	
4-5	1	1	1
3-3.5	2	2	4
2-2.9		2	2
	$\overline{3}$	$\overline{7}$	$\overline{8}$

45 For the three foods for which adequate retail price data were not available, the changes in *wholesale prices* between 1957-59 and 1965 were as follows: canned corn (sales promotion ratio 6.3%) −17%, lamb chops (3.0%) 12.7%, and turkey (3.0%) −6.6%.

ucts (butter 3.6%, fresh milk 2.8%), and rose more than the average for four products (American cheese 16.6%, pork 9.4%, veal 19.2%, and oranges 18.4%). Changes between a decline of 9.7% and an increase of 18.4% represent a wide range of experience and indicate that factors other than relative advertising and promotion costs were of primary importance.

The following tabulation summarizes the relationship between promotion to sales ratios and changes in 19 *wholesale* food prices between 1957-1959 and 1965:

Promotion as % of Sales	Changes In Wholesale Prices, 1957 – 1959 to 1965		
	Decline	Below Average Increase	Above Average Increase
6-7		2	1
4-5		2	1
3-3.5	6		4
2-2.9	1	1	1
	7	5	7

As compared with the increase of 5.1% in the wholesale price index for processed foods during this period, 7 of these prices declined, 5 rose less than the average, and 7 rose more than the average. In the 6 industries with promotion costs of 4% or more prices rose less than the average for 4 and more than the average for 2.

Clearly, there has been little relationship between the changes in food prices and promotion costs during the post-World War II period. For most of these products supply is the most important factor affecting price changes.

DRUG PRICES

1939-1966 From 1939 to 1965, the *wholesale prices* of drugs and pharmaceuticals (includes ethicals, proprietaries, and pharmaceutical materials) increased 71% or about one-half as much as the rise of 143% for all commodities. Between 1939 and 1947, wholesale prices for drug and pharmaceuticals rose more than the index for all commodities—103% as compared with 92%. However, the contrast in price trends since 1947 has been dramatic. In 1965, the prices of all drugs and pharmaceuticals were 16.2% *lower* than in 1947 as compared with the rise of 26.2% in the all-commodities index.

Most of this disparity developed between 1947 and 1955, when drugs and pharmaceuticals *fell* by 11.8% while the general index advanced 14.8%. These trends have continued since 1955 with a further decline of 4.9% and an increase of 10.0% respectively. Since the 1957-1959 period, the changes have been a decline of 1.9% for drugs and pharmaceuticals and an increase of 9.9% for the general index.

The U. S. Bureau of Labor Statistics included in its consumer price index for the period from 1939 to June 1964 an index of prescriptions and drugs that was based on three proprietary drugs: aspirin, milk of magnesia, and multiple vitamin concentrates. Between 1939 and June 1964, this index increased only 41.8% as compared with 123.1% for the entire CPI. Between the 1957-1959 base period and June 1964, the drug index *fell* by 1.3% as compared with the rise of 8.0% in the CPI.

Because the official index did not provide representative coverage for proprietaries, data were obtained for 18 products for which identical package sizes were available for three dates: May 1939, 1947, and early 1966 (see Appendix Table E-8).[46] Since volume data were not available to determine the relative importance of each product, the suggested retail prices of the 18 products were aggregated to determine how much it would have cost to buy one package of each in the three periods. The total was $12.80 in May 1939, $12.90 in 1947, and $17.12 in 1966. Thus, the aggregate price increased 33.8% between 1939 and early 1966 as compared with 132.4% for the entire CPI. Between 1939 and 1947, the price of only one of the 18 products rose while the CPI advanced 60.7%. Practically all (32.7%) of the increase in these drug prices took place in the postwar period.

For the years 1947 and 1966, prices were available on

---

46 The data for 1939 and 1947 originally were published in Backman, "Economics of Proprietary Drugs," *op. cit.*, pp. 888-90.

a consistent basis for five additional products (see Appendix Table E-8). Total suggested retail prices for one package of each of these five products was $2.65 in 1947 and $3.61 in 1966. The increase of 36.2% was in line with that for the 18 products cited earlier.

Clearly, there has been a modest rise in the retail prices of proprietaries during the past quarter of a century and since the end of World War II. The foregoing comparisons are particularly interesting because many of the items will be recognized as heavily advertised drug products.

Summary and Conclusions

Cost-price-volume relationships are very complex. To the extent advertising is successful, total sales volume expands and may result in reductions in unit costs for production and overhead. In such instances, *total unit costs* could be lower with heavy advertising than without it. In fact, for many new products, for which advertising costs are relatively the greatest, prices often decline—a trend which is made possible by the mass markets developed through various methods including advertising.[47]

On the other hand, in the declining phase of the life cycle of a product, unit costs would tend to rise as demand declines. Under such conditions, it is usually impossible to recover these rising costs out of higher prices. Clearly, each situation must be examined separately to determine the impact on unit costs.

The assumption that relatively high advertising costs necessarily must lead to higher prices reflects a misunderstanding of the pricing process. Although cost is one factor influencing prices, cost alone does not determine prices. It follows that a small component of total costs, such as advertising, usually will not play an influential role in setting prices.

It is sometimes suggested that a price reduction would

[47] Prices also may be reduced over time as a result of improved technology or an increase in competition rather than because of economies of scale.

be better for the customer and for the economy than an equivalent expenditure for advertising. This is an oversimplified statement. There is a time factor to be considered, since mass markets tend to be developed more quickly by the use of advertising which informs the consumer of the availability of new products. The informational aspects of advertising may contribute more to an expansion in demand than the lure of a lower price. Under such conditions, the ability to develop mass markets could be impaired if advertising were curtailed, and the end result could be higher rather than lower prices.

Price has a considerable appeal to many buyers. But the customer also is interested in many nonprice elements of a purchase. Unadvertised products often have little widespread appeal even though the price is lower. In fact, the ability to sell unadvertised products on a price basis often depends upon effective advertising for that class of products. For this reason, such unadvertised products are sometimes referred to as "barnacle brands." If the advertising were abandoned, the effectiveness of the price appeal might be reduced significantly.

A special study has been made of the relationship between the intensity of advertising (as measured by the advertising-sales ratio) and changes in wholesale and retail prices. The most intensively advertised categories of products have tended to show smaller increases in price than less heavily advertised categories during the post-World War II price inflation. The postwar record of changes in wholesale and retail prices for broad groups of products and for selected foods and proprietary drugs reveals that there has been no relationship between the intensity of advertising expenditures and the magnitude of price increases.

These data indicate that heavy advertising expenditures did not create a degree of market power which gave the affected industries the freedom to raise prices substantially during this period of general price inflation. It may be asserted that these data merely show that the market power was unexerted but remains a threat in the future. However, the earlier discussion indicated that the theory that brands create excessive market power is a myth. The price experience reinforces this conclusion.

VI

Advertising and Profit Rates

The major objective of advertising is to expand sales and to increase profits. Successful campaigns achieve these objectives in whole or in part. But the objective of higher profits is not confined to advertising. Profits can and do increase as a result of many other factors. The goal of business is to make products and/or services which customers will buy in sufficient quantities and at prices which will enable a company to earn satisfactory profits. Marketing is an important part of the process, and advertising is only part of the total marketing effort. The role to be played by marketing will vary among companies and industries; the contribution of advertising to these programs also varies widely.

It is usually virtually impossible to separate the contribution made to total sales volume by the inherent merits of the product, the availability of adequate financial resources, the caliber of the management, general economic trends, research and development, marketing programs including advertising, consumers' habits, tastes, and incomes, and other factors. Profits also are affected by the relationship between volume and costs, programs designed to effectuate economies, and changes in tax rates.

Although some attempts have been made to relate the relative levels of profits to advertising expenditures, the available data are incomplete and unsatisfactory. It would be necessary to relate directly the advertising and profit rates for specific products[1] or families of products sold by a company in order to make meaningful comparisons. Since heavily advertised products generally are produced by multiproduct companies, the results of even such comparisons are heavily dependent upon how a company allocates overhead among various products, depreciation policies, and methods of inventory valuation. As a result, even company comparisons have limited usefulness, particularly if the company sells a variety of products subject to different intensities of advertising.

When comparisons are made on an industry basis the limitations are much greater, because industry totals reflect the diverse experience of the more successful as well as less successful companies[2] and reflect the growing tendencies of many companies to branch out into unrelated product lines. When Census data are used for such studies, the experience of several subindustries tends to be combined thus reducing still further the significance of the comparisons.

Factors Affecting Profit Rates

Above-average profits usually are attributed to factors other than advertising by most researchers. The more important causes have included:

[1] Data for profits earned on specific products or families of products are never published by multiproduct companies. In fact, accurate profit figures are almost impossible to determine for each product even for internal use. Usually, companies determine the direct costs incurred for a product in order to ascertain how much each product contributes to general overhead, sales costs, taxes, and profits.

[2] *Fortune* reported in 1962 that Procter and Gamble had a net income of 6.7% on domestic and foreign sales, Lever Brothers 2.5%, and Colgate 3.4%; on domestic business the average for Colgate was only 0.7%. "The Soap Wars: A Strategic Analysis," *op. cit.,* p. 198.

1] An above average rate of growth in an industry.[3] An important contribution to growth is made by large-scale investment in research and development with the accompanying flow of new products. Professor Robert M. Solow has stated: " . . . it is plausible enough and can be rigorously proved—that the faster the rate of technical progress the higher the rate of return."[4] Similarly, Dr. William S. Comanor concluded that "Profits [in the drug industry] have come to depend primarily on the firm's position in the innovative race . . ." and that this position depended in turn upon the extent of research and development which "has been stimulated to a considerable extent by competitive pressures."[5]

2] Restricted raw materials and secret technology.[6]

3] Economic concentration. Professor Bain concluded that " . . . there is a definite relationship of the degree of seller concentration in manufacturing industries to the size of the profit rate, such that high seller concentration tends to be connected with substantially higher rates of excess profit than does moderate or low seller concentration."[7]

4] Product differentiation supported by advertising. Dr. Comanor has stated that "The growth of effective product

3 See Jules Backman, *Chemical Prices, Productivity, Wages and Profits,* Manufacturing Chemists' Association, Inc., Washington, D.C., November 1964, pp. 61-62; Simon Whitney, *Antitrust Policies,* Vol. I, Twentieth Century Fund, New York, 1958, p. 247; Robin Marris, *The Economic Theory of Managerial Capitalism,* Macmillan and Co., Ltd., London, 1964, p. 251.

4 Robert M. Solow, *Capital Theory and the Rate of Return,* North-Holland Publishing Co., Amsterdam, 1963, p. 46. See also Backman, *op. cit.*

5 Comanor, *op. cit.,* pp. 375-76.

6 Roland P. Soule, "Chemical Industry's Problem: Slowing Profits," *Chemical and Engineering News,* August 14, 1961, p. 103.

7 Bain, *op. cit.,* p. 412. See also D. Schwartzman, "The Effect of Monopoly on Price," *Journal of Political Economy,* August 1959, pp. 352-62; Testimony of Norman R. Collins in *Economic Concentration,* Part 2, Hearings before the Subcommittee on Antitrust and Monopoly of the Committee on the Judiciary, United States Senate, 89th Cong., 1st Sess., April 1965, pp. 711-21; "The Structure of Food Manufacturing," *op. cit.,* Chap. VI. For a contra view see George J. Stigler, *Capital and Rates of Return in Manufacturing Industries,* National Bureau of Economic Research, Princeton University Press, Princeton, N.J., 1963, pp. 67-69.

differentiation has led to an appreciable increase in [drug] industry profits and their maintenance at a relatively high level . . . The crucial significance of product differentiation is that it provides *the primary barrier to entry* into the relevant therapeutic markets. Since effective entry normally requires some form of technical advance, *the cost and risk of research comprise an important part of this barrier.*[8] (Italics added.)

5] Government policy such as changes in tariffs, public works, and subsidies.

6] Risk involved.[9] It has been noted that " . . . profits . . . can be associated with the assumption of uninsurable risks stemming from both cyclical and structural changes in the economy."[10]

Turner Data

Donald F. Turner has stated that "Industries with high advertising outlays tended to earn profit rates which were about 50% higher than those which did not undertake a significant effort . . . it is likely that these additional gains represent monopoly rewards. They represent price levels which can be explained only on the basis of restrictions on competition."[11] This conclusion was based on average profit

8 Comanor, *op. cit.,* p. 380. See also Zacher, *op. cit.,* p. 586, Borden, *op. cit.,* p. 425 and "The Structure of Food Manufacturing," *op. cit.,* p. 200.

9 It has been reported that out of 124 grocery products introduced between 1954 and 1964, 27 were discontinued after test marketing, 10 after achieving limited distribution, and 11 after achieving full distribution. Buzzell and Nourse concluded "The results of the survey clearly support the generalization that product innovation is a *costly* and *risky* venture" (Their italics). Cited in "Grocery Manufacturing," *op. cit.,* p. 39. Booz, Allen, & Hamilton has reported that "Of all the dollars of new product expense, almost three-fourths go to unsuccessful products," *Management of New Products,* 1964, p. 11.

10 McConnell, *op. cit.,* p. 585.

11 Turner, *op. cit.,* p. 3. These estimates appear to have been based upon an unpublished (but distributed) paper by William S. Comanor and Thomas A. Wilson, *Market Structure, Advertising, and Market Performance,* 1966.

experience in the four years 1954-1957 in 41 consumer goods industries.

Although industries with a greater intensity of advertising tended to have somewhat higher profit rates, the difference was considerably smaller than the 50% margin cited above, unless the comparison is confined to the six industries which had advertising-sales ratios of more than 6%.

The data also showed that industries with low advertising-sales ratios may have high rates of return. Thus, 18 industries reported a return on invested capital of 9% or higher; nine industries with advertising-sales ratios of above 3% earned an average of 12.0% while nine industries with ratios below 3% had an average profit rate of 10.8%. This appears to be a modest difference, whatever the cause.

Clearly, the underlying data are inadequate to support Mr. Turner's broad conclusion that large-scale advertising expenditures led to large "monopoly rewards." Moreover, as was noted earlier, Census data are the least satisfactory to determine these relationships or to provide the basis for a definitive conclusion on this point.

Survey of 1964 and 1965 Experience

A study has been made of the experience of the 125 companies which were the largest advertisers in terms of dollars in 1964 and in 1965. Data were available for 111 companies for 1965 and 114 companies for 1964. The advertising to sales ratios for these companies have been related to their return on invested capital to determine to what extent more intensive advertising has been accompanied by larger rates of profits. The nature of these data is discussed in Appendix D.

Greater intensity of advertising has been accompanied by somewhat higher profit rates (Chart VI-1 shows the pattern for 1965). But the wide dispersion around the line of relationship is evident. The coefficient of correlation (r) was .345 while the coefficient of determination (r^2) was only .119. This latter ratio suggests that a little more than one-tenth of the difference in profits rates was attributable to the relative differences in[12] advertising-sales ratios.[13]

Because the 111-company sample is composed of the largest dollar spenders for advertising, a question may be raised whether these companies had a much higher average level of profits than did all big companies, thus limiting the significance of comparisons within the group. Data published by *Fortune* and the First National City Bank for large companies may be used to answer this question.

CHART VI-1
Advertising Expenditures as a Percent of Sales and Return on Invested Capital for 111 Large Advertisers, 1965

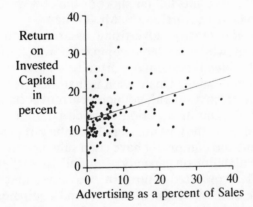

1] The 111 companies had a moderately higher average profit rate than did Fortune's 500 largest industrial companies. The *weighted average* was 13.6% for the 111 companies in the survey as compared with 13.0% for the 500 largest industrial companies.

12 The study of 114 companies in 1964 revealed similar relationships since r was .315 and r² was .099.

13 For 1964, the 114 companies had an average profit rate of 12.6% as compared with 12.1% for Fortune's 500 largest industrial companies.

2] The average return on net assets for the 102 *manufacturing* companies[14] included in this study was 14.7% in 1965 as compared with 13.8% for 2,298 leading manufacturing companies reported by the First National City Bank of New York.[15] These modest differences in profit returns are not necessarily all attributable to the effects of advertising. At the most it can be said that manufacturing companies with large dollar advertising expenditures reported profits that were 0.9 percentage point higher than the average for leading manufacturing companies. The relationships in 1964 were about the same.[16]

These data indicate that companies with large dollar expenditures for advertising have not earned much more on invested capital than leading manufacturing corporations generally. These results fall far short of the 50% differential attributed to heavy advertising by Mr. Turner.

Finally, if intensive advertising assures much higher rates of return, why don't large companies, which often are seeking profitable investment opportunities, move into these industries to earn them? One reason is that these returns are based on historic investment, not upon current costs of plant and equipment. During a period of price inflation, such as that experienced in the past quarter of a century, replacement costs for plant and equipment have risen substantially.

The availability of capacity acquired in earlier years tends to inflate reported returns in two ways: first the reported value of the investment in plant and equipment does not reflect the higher current cost and thus holds down total net worth or invested capital and second, reported earnings

14 Included in the survey for both years were nine non-manufacturing companies: American Telephone, Sears Roebuck, Columbia Broadcasting System, and six airlines.

15 *Monthly Economic Letter,* First National City Bank, New York, April 1966, p. 41.

16 In 1964, the 105 manufacturing companies included in the survey had a profit rate of 13.6% as compared with 12.6% for the leading manufacturers reported by the First National City Bank or a difference of 1.0 percentage point.

tend to be overstated because depreciation charges are based on those lower historic costs. The impact of these forces was recently determined in Great Britain for Unilever with the following dramatic effects:[17]

Unilever Ltd., 1965

	As Reported Historic Basis	Current Experience, Replacement Cost
Profit (before taxes) (000 £)	2,548	2,260
Estimated Capital (000 £)	10,797	13,780
Profit as Percent of Capital	23.6%	16.4%

The use of replacement cost reduced the before-tax rate of earnings by almost one-third. The meaningful figure for a new competitor in connection with this record is 16.4% before taxes, not 23.6%.

Differences in reported rates of profit also reflect other factors. Companies adopt different methods of depreciation or of costing for inventories, labor costs vary widely in relative importance, goodwill which is not recorded on the books varies in importance,[18] and rates of growth are different. In light of these factors, it is not too meaningful to attribute differences in profit rates to a single factor such as advertising.

Summary and Conclusions

Profit rates are influenced by many factors including new products developed by investment in research and development, technological changes, growth rates, general economic trends, caliber of management, government policy,

17 "Household Detergents," *op. cit.,* p. 19.

18 Good-will probably is of relatively greater importance for companies with intensive advertising, and hence the failure to include it in net worth would have a greater tendency to inflate rates of return than in other industries.

risks involved, and sales promotion policies. It is impossible to segregate the impact of each of these factors.

Intensive advertising tends to be accompanied by higher reported profit rates. However, the difference in return among companies with varying rates of advertising intensity tends to be moderate. The special study of the experience of 114 large advertisers in 1964 and 111 in 1965 showed that differences in *relative* advertising expenditures explained about one-tenth of the difference in profit rates.

The charge that large "monopoly rewards" accompany intensive advertising receives no support from these data. And this is not surprising. Intensive advertising assures no permanent advantages to the advertiser. The position at the top is precarious, not secure. Competitive pressures are constantly eroding the position of leading brands despite continued large-scale expenditures for advertising. That this development is not accompanied by a marked differential in profit rates is to be expected. The investment in advertising appears to yield a modest return in light of the risks of failure assumed.

VII

Summary and Conclusions

The charge that advertising is anticompetitive was described earlier as moving from 1] the "power of the purse" to 2] barriers to entry to 3] economic concentration to 4] monopolistic prices to 5] excessively high profits. This chain is broken at several points as the preceding analysis has shown.

1] Large companies have the "power of the purse" as well as other financial and nonfinancial advantages as compared with smaller companies.

2] Nevertheless, this financial power usually has not acted as an effective barrier to entry, particularly by other large companies. Moreover, the availability of local and regional advertising media at much lower costs than national media has been more important to smaller companies because so many markets are local in nature. Even where advertising may create a barrier to entry, this does not mean a barrier to competition.

Practically all markets are an amalgam of elements of monopoly and of competition. The possession of the monopoly of a brand is not the totality of the market situation. National brands must meet the competition of other national brands, substitute products, private brands, local or regional brands, and products sold solely on a price basis. The dynamic, competitive nature of these markets is underlined by the marked changes in brand shares, the successes achieved by many new national brands and private brands against so-called entrenched brands, and the inability of well-known and financially strong companies successfully to establish new brands at will. These developments indicate that the degree of market power, which supposedly accompanies product differentiation identified by brand names and implemented by large-scale advertising, is much weaker than claimed and is usually outweighed by competitive pressures.

3] There has been no relationship between the extent of economic concentration and the intensity of advertising as measured by advertising-sales ratios. In most industries, the composition of the Big Fours has changed over time as smaller companies have grown in size and have taken the competitive measure of their larger rivals. Smaller companies often have been especially alert to the opportunities created when new products have been developed. The Big Fours have not been exclusive clubs. New entrants to the market have successfully breached the citadel. The top as reflected in the Big Four has proved to be slippery in all but a few markets.

4] No relationship is found between advertising-sales ratios and changes in prices during the post-World War II period. Cost-price-volume relationships are very complex and change over the life cycle of a product. Prices are determined by many factors other than costs. Even where costs play a role, an expenditure of 5% to 15 % of total costs for advertising would not be the determinant of prices. Moreover, advertising costs are not net. If they were eliminated, other marketing costs would be incurred and in many instances the selling job would be done less efficiently or at higher cost.

Companies which allegedly have developed strong market power for their brands through heavy advertising and as a result have been insulated from price competition generally have been unable to exploit the postwar price inflation by above-average price hikes. Rather, the companies with the greatest intensity of advertising often recorded less than average increases or even decreases in prices. This development is not at all surprising in light of the competitive ferment described earlier.

5] Companies with relatively high advertising-sales ratios tend to have somewhat higher profit rates than less intensive advertisers. These higher profits appear to reflect the larger volume resulting from successful advertising rather than the exercise of market power to charge high monopolistic prices. The investment in advertising appears to yield a modest return in light of the risks of failure assumed.

The alleged flow of control from the "power of the purse" to "excessive profits," therefore, is not supported by the available evidence. The barrier to entry created by large financial requirements is weak. The relationship between advertising intensity and high economic concentration is nonexistent. There appears to be no link between advertising intensity and price increases. Intensive advertisers appear to have only moderately higher profit rates than other companies. The record shows clearly that advertising is highly competitive, not anticompetitive.

In the process of analyzing the competitive effects of advertising, its contributions to the economy also have been noted. Some economic waste may be involved when large-scale advertising is accompanied by a "shuffling around" of volume. However, such advertising, rather than being wasteful, may make an affirmative contribution to a better and fuller use of resources in an economy operating at less-than-capacity levels. In any event, some duplication and hence waste is unavoidable in a competitive economy. The real question is do the benefits of competition outweigh such costs? The following benefits of advertising must be underlined as an offset to any economic waste involved.

1] Advertising contributes to economic growth and hence to an expanded number of job opportunities. The development of new and improved products has contributed to the growth of our economy. The discovery of a new product or the improvement of an existing one adds nothing to economic activity until markets are developed. Because management is fully aware of the availability of advertising and other marketing tools, it goes ahead with large investments in research and development. The incentive to introduce these products is the profit to be derived from the development of mass markets. This is the job of advertising.

2] The creation of mass markets through advertising may contribute to the economies of mass production. The result has been an ever-larger supply of goods at prices within the range of the consumer's pocketbook. In many instances, the economies are so large that the price is lower than it would be if the advertising expenditures had not been incurred. The greater availability of goods has contributed significantly to a rise in levels of living for the average family.

3] The expenditures for advertising do not represent a net cost to the economy, however that cost is measured. Part of these funds make it possible to finance a wide selection of magazines and newspapers of all shades of opinion[1] as well as to provide radio and television entertainment.[2] As Secretary of Commerce John T. Connor has reported: " . . . none would be within prices most people could pay were it not that advertising underwrites the principal costs."[3] Despite some criticism of the power of advertisers, we are likely to have a more independent press when it is financed through advertising than when it is subsidized or completely controlled by the government, as the experience in many countries unfortunately has demonstrated.

1 In 1963, advertising accounted for 71.1% of the total receipts of newspapers and 66.5% for periodicals. U.S. Department of Commerce, Bureau of the Census, *Statistical Abstract of the United States: 1966,* Washington, D.C., 1966, p. 522.

2 No effort has been made in this study to evaluate the quality of this entertainment.

3 An Address Before The Cleveland Advertising Club, Statler-Hilton Hotel, Cleveland, Ohio, September 28, 1966.

4] By preselling the customer, new and more economical methods of distribution have been made possible. Vending machines, supermarkets, and discount houses provide good illustrations. Since there has been considerable concern about the "high cost of distribution," a reduction in these costs is an important plus factor for advertising. Moreover, companies are constantly checking the effectiveness of alternative means of marketing. The selection of advertising to do the job indicates that businessmen believe it to be the most efficient method to achieve sales objectives. To the extent that this is true, advertising results in a more efficient use of resources — a direct contradiction of the "waste" argument.

5] Product differentiation as reflected in brands makes it possible for the consumer to identify the manufacturer. Thus, it becomes vital to establish and to maintain high standards of quality which the buyer then associates with the brand. In fact, it often is necessary to improve the quality in order to differentiate it from competitive products. While some economic waste may develop as a result of creating trivial product differences, there also are benefits which flow from improved products.

6] Advertising provides a major source of information about old and particularly new products. Such communication plays a vital role in the effective operation of our economy. It saves the customer substantial amounts of time and effort, since he obtains information concerning the relative merits of competing products before he begins shopping.

Every piece of advertising does not lead to the above benefits. Certainly there is wide agreement that misleading advertising must be proscribed.[4] Nor can it be questioned that some advertising is in poor taste even though it is not

4 The Pure Food and Drug Administration and the Federal Trade Commission have authority to take action against misleading advertising. For a detailed description of the standards developed by the Federal Trade Commission in connection with false advertising see Ira M. Millstein, "The Federal Trade Commission and False Advertising," *Columbia Law Review*, March 1964, pp. 450-99.

misleading. Nevertheless, on balance, it seems clear that advertising makes a major contribution to our national economic well-being and to the competitive nature of our economy.

Appendix A

Advertising in the National Economy

The growth in total advertising expenditures (Appendix Table A-1) has corresponded closely to the growth in the major measures of aggregate economic activity such as Gross National Product, Personal Consumption Expenditures, Disposable Personal Income, and Total Corporate Sales. (Appendix Table A-2) Advertising expenditures as a percentage of each aggregate are shown in Appendix Table A-3. The increases in each of the national economic aggregates adjusted for price changes and converted to 1958 dollars are shown in Appendix Table A-4. Appendix Table A-5 summarizes the statistical relationships between advertising and the several economic aggregates. Appendix Table A-6 compares the data published by IRS, *Printers' Ink,* and *Advertising Age.* The changing relative importance of various types of advertising expenditures is shown in Appendix Tables A-7 and A-8.

Printers' Ink Data

Printers' Ink has published annual data for total advertising expenditures and for expenditures in eight recognized media—radio, newspapers,[1] magazines, television,

1 Advertising in weekly newspapers is included in the miscellaneous

farm publications, business papers, outdoor advertising and direct mail—annually since 1935. (See Appendix Table A-1) In 1965, the total amount spent for these eight types of media advertising was $12.3 billion.

In addition, there is included a miscellaneous category which originally was estimated by Professor Neil Borden to be about 20% of total advertising expenditures. *Printers' Ink* has continued to use this same relative proportion for miscellaneous. It has never made available publicly any breakdown of the miscellaneous category. According to *Printers' Ink* the "proportion was initially arrived at by estimating the percent of the average advertiser's total budget not covered by the eight media listed in the table."[2]

According to Professor Borden, the cost of administration of advertising departments of business firms was about 10% of the total advertising expenditures or about half of the miscellaneous total.[3] 10% of total expenditures is equal to 12-½% of media expenditures.[4] Other expenditures included under miscellaneous are advertising in weekly newspapers, point-of-purchase materials, transportation advertising,[5] and "all other legitimate advertising expenditures not already covered."[6] It is also reported that when

---

total. *Advertising Age* began publishing annual estimates in 1965. The series is available yearly since 1947. The total for 1965 was $15,570 million as compared with the PI total of $15,255 million. The *Advertising Age* data, compiled by Dr. Charles Yang, provide a different breakdown of the components, since it allocates part of the total to agency costs and also reports a breakdown by major industrial classifications. *Advertising Age,* June 13, 1966, p. 82.

2 Printers' Ink, *Advertisers Guide to Marketing for 1960,* October 30, 1959, p. 306.

3 Borden, *op. cit.,* p. 913.

4 Media expenditures average about 80% of total advertising expenditures. Thus, 10% of the total is equal to 1/8 of media or 12½%.

5 Starting with 1963, transit advertising which was formerly included in miscellaneous has been reported separately. The 1965 total was $33 million. It has been included in the miscellaneous total to have a consistent series in Appendix Table A-1.

6 Printers' Ink, *Guide to Marketing for 1963,* p. 384.

revisions are made in the data for the eight major media, "the miscellaneous totals are usually changed to absorb the effect of the revisions in other media so that the grand totals are left unchanged."[7]

The miscellaneous total has increased from $398 million in 1940 to $2,979 million in 1965 or more than sevenfold. On the basis of the Borden estimates, about $200 million of the total advertising expenditures in 1940 and about $1,500 million of the 1965 total would be for corporate advertising departments. This would appear to be a completely unrealistic figure which would result in an overstatement of total advertising expenditures.

Cost of Advertising Departments

It is not probable that when total advertising expenditures increased 7-½ times, corporate advertising overhead would have increased in the same ratio.[8] It should be kept in mind that a significant part of the increase in total advertising expenditures reflected greater exposure for an advertisement when circulation or potential listening audiences increased. The additional cost for greater exposure should not be accompanied by a comparable rise in the cost of corporate advertising departments.

To determine the relative costs of running an advertising department in relation to media expenditures and the trend of these costs over time, an inquiry was addressed to a small number of companies. Scattered data were obtained from 14 companies with total advertising expenditures of $873 million in 1965.

In terms of the dollar volume of advertising, these companies were distributed among the 125 largest advertisers as follows:

7 *Ibid.*, pp. 384-85.

8 A study of British advertising showed that when total expenditures rose from £ 308.8 million in 1956 to £ 501.5 million in 1963, the cost of "administration" rose from £ 21.0 million to £ 27.0 million but the *relative cost fell* from 6.8% to 5.4%. "Reith Report," *op. cit.*, p. 54. Administration appears to include the cost of advertising departments plus the cost of

Rank	No. of Companies in Sample
1-10	4
11-20	2
21-30	0
31-40	1
41-50	0
51-60	3
61-70	0
71-80	0
81-90	1
91-100	2
Below 125	1
	14

The data are summarized below:

Relationship of Costs of Advertising Departments to Total Media Expenditures For Selected Companies, 1955, 1960, 1965

Company	1955	1960	1965
		(percent)	
A	N.A.	6.0	5.5
B	2.0	0.9	1.2
C	N.A.	N.A.	0.5
D	5.0	7.5	6.0
E	N.A.	1.9	1.3
F	11.0	7.0	7.0
G	N.A.	5.0	6.0
H	2.5	2.7	1.7
I	0.8	0.4	0.8
J	1.5	2.1	3.8
K	3.9	5.0	5.6
L	19.5	14.0	12.0
M	N.A.	N.A.	4.0
N	2.3	1.9	1.2

N.A. not available

12 companies furnished data for 1960 and 1965: 6 showed

---

advertising consultants. Nicholas Kaldor and Rodney Silverman, *A Statistical Analysis of Advertising Expenditure and of the Revenue of the Press,* Cambridge University Press, Cambridge, England, 1948, pp. 8, 107, 110-11.

a decline in relative costs, 1 was unchanged, and 5 reported increases. Data for only 9 companies were available for 1955 and 1965: 5 reported declines, 1 was unchanged, and 3 reported increases in the relative costs of operating their advertising departments over the 10-year period.

The weighted average cost of the advertising departments of the 14 companies was 3.7% of their media expenditures. Only 1 company had a ratio in excess of 10%.

While these data may not be representative they do suggest 1] some tendency for the relative costs of corporate advertising departments to decline as volume increases and 2] the strong probability that the relative cost is significantly lower than 12-½% of total media expenditures, the proportion reported by Professor Borden for the pre-World War II period. In light of these data, it seems clear that further research is required to determine the nature of the miscellaneous items because they appear to result in some overestimation of the annual cost of advertising.

Advertising Age Data

These data are available since 1947. (See Appendix Table A-6) The *Advertising Age* data also have a large composite, "other expenditures" which has averaged 25 to 27% of the total. Charles Y. Yang, who compiled these data, concluded that "Since the figures were derived as residuals between the total receipts from the sources and the total expenditures in all the major allocation categories—for which independent estimates were made—the accuracy of estimation must rely on the consistency in the proportion of the total money expended in this category every year. If these percentages are stable, as was found, we can be assured of the accuracy of the estimates."[9]

None of the major media has accounted for a constant ratio of total advertising expenditures. It is difficult, there-

9 Charles Y. Yang, "Input-Output Concept Is Basis of Improved Estimates on Advertising Expenditures in the U.S.," *Advertising Age,* March 29, 1965, p. 82. Dr. Yang's estimates cited in this section were derived from this article.

fore, to understand why the "other expenditures" ratio should remain unchanged over the years. As it is probable that the components of the "other" category have changed in relative importance, it would be a most unusual coincidence if the changes within this category were exactly offsetting.

Moreover, the conclusion is also based upon the assumption that Dr. Yang's estimates of total advertising expenditures are accurate. To the extent that they are too high or too low, the residual, "other expenditures" will also be affected. Dr. Yang derived his totals by adding to the Internal Revenue Service corporate data estimates for unincorporated business. His basic assumption was that "For any given industry the average behavior of a group of companies with regard to advertising spending is not likely to be affected significantly by the type of establishment (whether incorporated or unincorporated) if their sizes are roughly equal."[10]

This proposition is stated as a fact, although no evidence is offered to support it.[11] The *Advertising Age* total was $2,528 million *greater* than the IRS total. This seems to be a rather large total for unincorporated business. For example, it may be questioned whether the large number of Mom and Pop stores spend much, if anything, for advertising.[12] Yet, to the IRS total of $2,221 million for retailing, he added $849 million for unincorporated business in 1962.[13] These questions are being raised to emphasize the inadequate basis

10 *Ibid.*, p. 80.

11 The Federal Trade Commission found that in food manufacturing, unincorporated companies "are small firms with little or no advertising." "The Structure of Food Manufacturing", *op. cit.*, p. 63.

12 According to Dr. Yang, sole proprietorships in retailing had an average volume of $41,700 in 1961, to which he applied a ratio of 0.98% for advertising. This was the ratio he found for corporations with average sales of $56,000. *Op. cit.*, p. 79. It is doubtful that stores with average sales of only $41,700 annually spent 1% of these sales for advertising.

13 For 1962, Dr. Yang's total for services exceeded the IRS total by $730 million, for construction by $113 million, for wholesale trade by $173 million, and for agriculture, forestry, and fisheries by $124 million. These industries all have a substantial number of noncorporate enterprises.

for the conclusion that consistency of residuals derived from such data proves anything.

Printers' Ink and *Advertising Age* have made a major contribution and performed a real service in compiling the data for advertising expenditures. However, these data can be improved.

The above brief discussion indicates that a real effort should be made—both by *Printers' Ink* and *Advertising Age*—to break down the miscellaneous total into its constituent parts so that the real significance of the reported aggregates can be determined. Because 20% may have been a proper estimate for miscellaneous expenditures when the total advertising expenditures were $2 billion does not provide a warrant for continuing to use this ratio when the total exceeds $15 billion. This is an important weakness in the available data. Because of their value, the advertising community should cooperate in making available the information required to improve these data.

Internal Revenue Service Data

Data showing expenditures by *corporations* for advertising are also published by the Internal Revenue Service—usually after a lag of several years.[14] These data are available starting with 1945. As Appendix Table A-6 shows, there has been a persistent disparity over the years, with IRS totals running lower than PI. In 1962, IRS reported total *corporate* advertising expenditures at $10.4 billion as compared with $12.4 billion for total advertising expenditures by *Printers' Ink,* or a difference of $2 billion.

This difference reflects any overstatement in the cost of corporate advertising departments and unincorporated business and personal classified advertisements, neither

14 Thus, the latest data available at the time of this study was for the fiscal year 1962-1963, which essentially covers the calendar year 1962. Dr. Yang reported that in "the 1958-1959 tax period, 89.6% of total business receipts of corporations originated in the calendar year of 1958." Yang, *op. cit.,* p. 82.

of which is included in the IRS totals. It may also reflect varying practices by corporations in reporting the costs of their advertising departments,[15] and the treatment of point-of-purchase materials,[16] which may be included by some corporations as promotion rather than as advertising in their reports to IRS.

Finally, some part of the direct-mail total represents charitable fund solicitations which also are not included in the IRS data. *Expenditures by charitable organizations, government advertising, and personal classified ads would have to be excluded from the Printers' Ink total to obtain a more accurate picture of business spending for advertising.*

The IRS data *understate* business expenditures for advertising by the amounts spent by unincorporated business. The *Printers' Ink* data *overstate* actual business spending for advertising to the extent that it includes government expenditures, personal classified advertisements, and fund-raising appeals and to the extent it overstates the cost of corporate advertising departments. The actual spending, which lies between these two totals, cannot be determined. *Printers' Ink* data will be used to determine relationships to national aggregates, since they are available on a more current basis. Moreover, since the *Printers' Ink* series is available since 1935, a longer-term relationship can be derived than by using the *Advertising Age* series, which is available only since 1947, or IRS data, available since 1945.

Advertising and National Economic Aggregates

The relationship between advertising expenditures and

15 A Federal Trade Commission study has suggested that " . . . some corporations apparently include only the direct advertising expenditures, and exclude indirect expenditures such as advertising allowances given to retailers" in their reports to IRS. "The Structure of Food Manufacturing," *op. cit.,* p. 63, FN. 5.

16 For 1962, total expenditures for point-of-purchase displays were estimated to be $416 million. *Advertising Age,* June 13, 1966, p. 82.

the economic aggregates can be illustrated by the use of scatter charts. For example, Chart II-1 in the text is a scatter diagram showing the relationship between advertising expenditures and total personal consumption expenditures (PCE) (Charts A-1, A-2 and A-3 in this Appendix show the relationships between advertising expenditures and the other economic aggregates). Each dot in the chart represents the relationship between advertising expenditures and PCE for a single year. If we drop a vertical line from a particular point, the intersection of this vertical line with the horizontal axis gives PCE for that year. The intersection of the horizontal line drawn from the point to the vertical axis gives the corresponding advertising expenditures for that year.

A straight line through the scatter points gives a rough approximation of the "average" relationship between advertising expenditures and PCE. The average relationship has been determined mathematically.[17] The slope of the line drawn through the scatter points in Chart II-1 shows the increase in advertising expenditures per dollar of increase in personal consumption expenditures. For each dollar increase in personal consumption expenditures "on the average," there has been an increase in advertising expenditures of 3.8 cents.

Appendix Table A-5 shows the results of least squares regressions (the line of relationship) for the years 1935-65 and for those same years excluding World War II and the Korean War. Advertising expenditures are related to the four different economic aggregates shown in column 2. Column 3 shows the increase in advertising expenditures per dollar increase in the economic aggregate. For example, during this 30-year period a dollar increase in corporate

17 For detailed information about statistical techniques see Ernest Kurnow, Gerald J. Glasser and Frederick R. Ottman, *Statistics for Business Decisions,* Richard D. Irwin, Inc., Homewood, Ill., 1959. See also Frederick E. Croxton and Dudley J. Cowden, *Practical Business Statistics,* Third Edition, Prentice-Hall, Englewood Cliffs, New Jersey, 1960.

sales has been associated with an increase of 1.52 cents in advertising expenditures.

Column 4 shows that with one exception, on the average, the ratio of advertising expenditures to the economic aggregates increases slightly with advances in the aggregates over the years covered. For example, the largest increase in the ratio is between advertising and disposable personal income; the increase of $400 billion in DPI between 1939 and 1965 was accompanied by a rise of about 0.42 of one percentage point in the advertising-sales ratio. (See Appendix Tables A-2 and A-3.)

Finally, column 5 shows the coefficient of determination

CHART A-1
Relationship between Advertising and Gross National Product, 1935-1965

Advertising Expenditures in Billions of Dollars

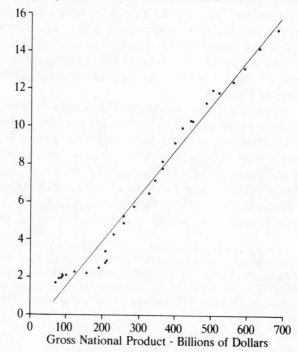

Gross National Product - Billions of Dollars

(r^2). The coefficient of determination indicates the percentage of the variation in advertising expenditures which may be "explained" by variations in the economic aggregates. In all cases, r^2 is very close to 1.0, thus indicating excellent fits. The fits are somewhat better when the war years are excluded. This is understandable, since advertising expenditures were relatively depressed during World War II.

Thus, from 97.7% to 99.1% of the variation in advertising expenditures may be explained by variations in the various economic aggregates. The relationship to corporate sales is slightly better than the other three.

CHART A-2
Relationship between Advertising
and Disposable Personal Income, 1935-1965

Advertising Expenditures
in Billions of Dollars

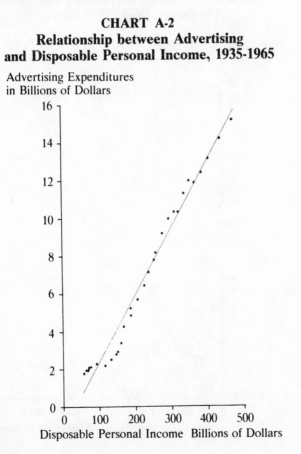

Disposable Personal Income Billions of Dollars

The historical interactions of many factors have resulted in such a close relationship between advertising expenditures and economic aggregates over a span of 30 years that it seems fairly safe to assume that the relationship is likely to continue for some time in the future. Thus, for example, if gross national product and personal consumption expenditures are projected for a future year, advertising expenditures can be estimated for that year.

CHART A-3

Relationship between Advertising and Total Corporate Sales, 1935-1965

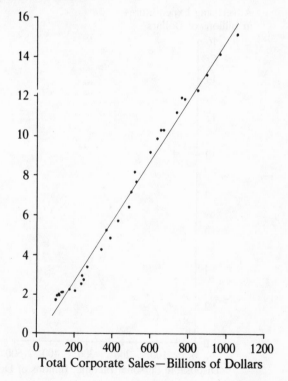

Advertising Expenditures
in Billions of Dollars

Total Corporate Sales—Billions of Dollars

Finally, the numbers in parenthesis in column 3 of Appendix Table A-5 show the standard errors. A small standard error relative to the regression estimate implies more confidence in the relationship shown than a large standard error. Appendix Table A-5 shows that the standard error for the 1.52 cents increase in advertising per dollar rise in corporate sales is 0.03 cents for the years 1935-65. If we add two standard errors to 1.52 cents and also subtract two standard errors, we have a range of 1.46 cents and 1.58 cents. These two numbers constitute "a confidence interval about the estimate." It can be stated that there are 95 chances out of 100 that the estimated increase in advertising expenditures per dollar rise in corporate sales is likely to lie somewhere within this confidence interval.

Relative Importance of Advertising

The relative importance of advertising in our national economy is indicated on various bases below:

	Advertising as Percent 1965
Personal consumption expenditures	3.54%
Disposable personal income	3.25
Gross national product	2.24

Advertising expenditures were equivalent to about 2.3% of GNP just before World War II and 2.2% in the first half of the 1960's. (See Appendix Table A-3.) This comparison suggests that advertising is a little less important in the national economy now than in the prewar years.[18] However, because of the increasing share of output consumed by government, there are several limitations to using GNP as a comparative. In 1935, government accounted for 13.9% of total GNP, in 1950 it was 13.3%, and in 1965 it was 19.9%.

18 Some writers emphasize this relationship. See Daniel Starch, *Measuring Advertising Leadership and Results,* McGraw-Hill Book Co., New York, 1966, pp. 244-45.

As a result, comparisons of advertising with total GNP currently tend to yield a lower ratio relative to earlier years when government was a less important factor.

Since advertising generally is directed to individual consumers, the more meaningful comparisons are with disposable personal income and personal consumption expenditures. However, a small proportion of advertising is intended for sales to other businesses[19] and hence the ratios to disposable personal income and personal consumption expenditures overstate to a small extent the relative importance of consumer advertising.

In the 1960's total advertising expenditures have been equal to about 3.5% of personal consumption expenditures[20] as compared with about 3.0% just prior to World War II and 2.7% to 3.0% in 1929.[21] (See Chart A-4) During the war years the proportion fell to about 2.5%. In the early postwar years, the proportion increased steadily but did not return to the prewar level of 3.0% until 1950, when the wartime shortages of automobiles and other durable goods had been largely met and vigorous sales competition restored.

During the 1950's, advertising grew faster than consumer incomes and outlays, the ratio increasing from 3.0% in 1950 to 3.6% in 1960. In the latter half of that decade, the total fluctuated between 3.6% and 3.7% of personal consumption expenditures, largely because of the burgeoning expenditures for television. Television advertising increased from .09% to .49% of personal consumption expenditures. Thus, even excluding television advertising, there was an increase from 2.90% to 3.18%. In connection with this reported rise in the relative importance of advertising two points must be kept in mind. To the extent that the total expenditures re-

19 In 1965, 4.9% of total advertising expenditures was in business papers.

20 National advertising expenditures were about 2% of personal consumption expenditures.

21 Dr. Blank estimated total advertising expenditures in 1929 at $2.1 to $2.4 billion. "A Note on the Golden Age of Advertising," *op. cit.,* p. 37.

ported for advertising are too high because of the method of calculation, discussed earlier, the increase in the ratio may be smaller than reported. However, as incomes have expanded, a considerable part of the increase has been available for optional consumption.

Spending for the necessities of life does not rise as rapidly as income and hence a growing proportion of the rise has been available for those items that make for a better life. For example, the Conference Board has estimated that discretionary purchasing power increased from $69 billion in 1946 to $207 billion in 1965.[22] This sharp rise in discretionary income provided an enlarged market potential for both new and old products and a strong inducement for more advertising to convert this potential demand into actual sales.

CHART A-4

Advertising Expenditures as a Percent of Personal Consumption Expenditures, Selected Years, 1929-1965

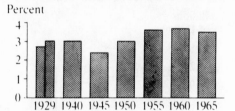

Local and National Advertising

A substantial part of the media advertising is local in nature, largely by retail stores and small local establishments. *Printers' Ink* identified the following expenditures for local advertising in 1965:

	millions
Newspaper	$3,587.1
Radio	569.0
Television	411.0
Outdoor	59.9
Total	$4,627.0

22 *Discretionary Spending,* Technical Paper, Number 17, National Industrial Conference Board, New York, 1966, p. 35.

Total media advertising *locally* was $4,627 million in 1965; national advertising aggregated $7,633 million.[23] Of course, all of these national expenditures were not for consumer goods. For example, advertising in business papers alone amounted to $671 million in 1965. Excluding these expenditures, the national total is reduced to $6,962 million; some part of this latter total is not for consumer goods[24] Thus, it appears that expenditures for national media advertising for consumer goods were considerably less than $7 billion in 1965.[25]

Despite the sharp increase in dollar expenditures for local advertising, it has declined in relative importance during the past quarter of a century. (See Chart A-5.)

This decline developed largely between 1940 and 1960.[26]

CHART A-5
Media Advertising: Total and Local, 1940 1950, 1960, and 1965

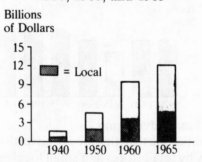

Billions of Dollars

23 *Printers' Ink* allocates the miscellaneous expenditures between national and local largely on the basis of the expenditures for media advertising. On this basis, the total in 1965 was national, $9,365 million, and local, $5,890 million.

24 Dr. David M. Blank has estimated that " . . . less than 10 percent of all national advertising in major media other than business papers is not devoted to consumer goods or services." Blank, *op. cit.,* p. 38, fn. 9.

25 If the miscellaneous total is allocated to national advertising, the total is about $8.6 billion.

26 To a large extent this trend has been due to the growth of television. Excluding television the local share was 42.2% in 1950, 41.9% in 1960, and 43.3% in 1965.

Media Advertising

	Total	Local	Percent Local
	(millions)		
1940	$1,690	$ 723	42.8
1950	4,585	1,917	41.8
1960	9,603	3,641	37.9
1965	12,276	4,627	37.7

There has been little change in the relative importance of local advertising since 1958, with the proportion averaging around 38%. Total national advertising excluding business papers has increased as follows:

	millions
1940	$ 891
1950	2,417
1960	5,353
1965	6,978

The major criticisms have been directed at national advertising of consumer goods and hence are concerned with far smaller amounts than the total for all advertising expenditures.

Appendix Table A-1
Advertising Expenditures 1935-1966
(Millions of Dollars)

Year	Maga-zines	News-papers	Farm Pub.	Radio Net-work	Radio Spot	Radio Local	Television Net-work	Television Spot	Television Local	Direct Mail	Out-door	Business Papers	Misc.*	Total
1935	136	762	4	63	15	35				282	31	51	312	1,690
1936	162	844	4	76	23	24				319	38	61	353	1,902
1937	193	873	7	89	28	48				333	44	70	388	2,072
1938	169	782	3	89	34	44				324	43	61	356	1,904
1939	180	793	6	99	35	50				333	44	69	372	1,980
1940	198	815	7	113	42	60				334	45	76	398	2,088
1941	214	844	7	125	52	70				353	53	89	430	2,236
1942	199	798	6	129	59	73				329	44	98	422	2,156
1943	275	900	9	157	71	86				322	42	142	493	2,496
1944	324	888	11	192	87	114				326	56	177	549	2,724
1945	365	921	12	198	92	134				290	72	204	587	2,875
1946	427	1,158	14	200	98	157				334	86	211	680	3,364
1947	493	1,475	20	201	106	199				579	121	233	833	4,260
1948	513	1,750	20	211	121	230				689	132	251	947	4,864
1949	493	1,916	21	203	123	245	29	9	19	756	131	248	1,010	5,202
1950	515	2,076	21	196	136	273	85	31	55	803	143	251	1,125	5,710
1951	574	2,258	26	180	138	289	181	70	82	924	149	292	1,265	6,426
1952	616	2,473	29	162	142	321	256	94	104	1,024	162	365	1,409	7,156

Appendix Table A-1 (continued)

Year	Maga-zines	News-papers	Farm Pub.	Radio			Television			Direct Mail	Out-door	Busi-ness Papers	Misc.*	Total
				Net-work	Spot	Local	Net-work	Spot	Local					
1953	667	2,645	31	141	146	324	320	146	141	1,099	176	395	1,525	7,755
1954	668	2,695	32	114	135	309	422	207	180	1,202	187	408	1,604	8,164
1955	729	3,088	34	84	134	326	540	260	225	1,299	192	446	1,836	9,194
1956	795	3,236	36	61	161	346	625	329	253	1,419	201	496	1,948	9,905
1957	814	3,283	34	63	187	368	670	352	244	1,471	199	568	2,059	10,311
1958	767	3,193	34	58	190	372	709	397	248	1,589	192	525	2,030	10,302
1959	866	3,546	36	44	206	406	740	486	267	1,688	193	569	2,206	11,255
1960	941	3,703	35	43	222	428	783	527	281	1,830	203	609	2,328	11,932
1961	924	3,623	33	43	218	423	887	533	270	1,876	180	578	2,321	11,845
1962	973	3,681	34	46	229	461	976	611	311	1,933	171	597	2,359	12,381
1963	1,034	3,804	34	56	238	495	1,025	679	328	2,078	171	615	2,551	13,107
1964	1,108	4,148	33	59	251	537	1,132	780	377	2,184	175	623	2,750	14,155
1965	1,199	4,457	33	60	268	558	1,237	866	412	2,324	180	671	2,959	15,255
1966p	1,295	4,876	34	65	294	642	1,373	931	461	2,454	181	712	3,272	16,545

Sources: Printers' Ink, Guide to Marketing for 1963, August 31, 1962, pp. 384-85; February 11, 1966, p. 10, February 24, 1967.

*Apparently includes cost of corporate advertising departments, signs and advertising novelties, car cards, motion pictures, and art work, plates, and other mechanical costs. See Neil H. Borden, The Economic Effects of Advertising, Richard D. Irwin, Inc., Chicago, Ill., 1942, p.54.

Appendix Table A-2
National Economic Trends, 1929-1966
(Billions of Dollars)

	Total Gross National Product	Personal Consumption Expenditures	Disposable Personal Income	Total Corporate Sales
1929	103.1	77.2	83.3	138.6
1930	90.4	60.9	74.5	118.3
1931	75.8	60.5	64.0	92.4
1932	58.0	48.6	48.7	69.2
1933	55.6	45.8	45.5	73.0
1934	65.1	51.3	52.4	89.6
1935	72.2	55.7	58.5	102.0
1936	82.5	61.9	66.3	119.5
1937	90.4	66.5	71.2	128.9
1938	84.7	63.9	65.5	108.6
1939	90.5	66.8	70.3	120.8
1940	99.7	70.8	75.7	135.2
1941	124.5	80.6	92.7	176.2
1942	157.9	88.5	116.9	202.8
1943	191.6	99.3	133.5	233.4
1944	210.1	108.3	146.3	246.7
1945	212.0	119.7	150.2	239.5
1946	208.5	143.4	160.0	270.9
1947	231.3	160.7	169.8	347.8
1948	257.6	173.6	189.1	388.7
1949	256.5	176.8	188.6	370.1
1950	284.8	191.0	206.9	431.9
1951	328.4	206.3	226.6	488.4
1952	345.5	216.7	238.3	499.5
1953	364.6	230.0	252.6	523.3
1954	364.8	236.5	257.4	516.5
1955	398.0	254.4	275.3	599.4
1956	419.2	266.7	293.2	632.4
1957	441.1	281.4	308.5	671.8
1958	447.3	290.1	318.8	658.2
1959	483.6	311.2	337.3	739.4

Appendix Table A-2 (continued)

	Total Gross National Product	Personal Consumption Expenditures	Disposable Personal Income	Total Corporate Sales
1960	503.8	325.2	350.0	763.3
1961	520.1	335.2	364.4	780.8
1962	560.3	355.1	385.3	849.1
1963	590.5	375.0	404.6	892.6
1964	631.7	401.4	436.6	963.9
1965	681.2	431.5	469.1	1,056.8
1966	739.5	465.0	505.3	N.A.

Sources: Economic Report of the President, January 1967, Washington, D.C., 213, 229; U.S. Department of Commerce, Office of Business Economics, *National Income,* 1964 Edition, Washington, D.C., 1964, pp. 204-205; *U.S. Income and Output,* Washington, D.C., 1958, p. 215; *Survey of Current Business,* July 1962, p. 27, July 1964, p. 28, and July 1966, pp. 11, 18, 35.

Appendix Table A-3

Advertising Expenditures as Percent of Gross National Product, Personal Consumption Expenditures, Disposable Personal Income, and Total Corporate Sales, 1935-1966

	Gross National Product	Personal Consumption Expenditures	Disposable Personal Income	Total Corporate Sales
1935	2.34	3.03	2.89	1.66
1936	2.31	3.07	2.87	1.59
1937	2.29	3.12	2.91	1.61
1938	2.25	2.98	2.91	1.75
1939	2.19	2.96	2.82	1.64
1940	2.09	2.95	2.76	1.54
1941	1.80	2.77	2.41	1.27
1942	1.37	2.44	1.84	1.06
1943	1.30	2.51	1.87	1.07
1944	1.30	2.52	1.86	1.10
1945	1.36	2.40	1.91	1.20
1946	1.61	2.35	2.10	1.24
1947	1.84	2.65	2.51	1.22
1948	1.89	2.80	2.57	1.25
1949	2.03	2.94	2.76	1.41
1950	2.00	2.99	2.76	1.32
1951	1.96	3.11	2.84	1.32
1952	2.07	3.30	3.00	1.43
1953	2.13	3.37	3.07	1.48
1954	2.24	3.45	3.17	1.58
1955	2.31	3.61	3.34	1.53
1956	2.36	3.71	3.38	1.57
1957	2.34	3.66	3.34	1.53
1958	2.30	3.55	3.23	1.57
1959	2.33	3.62	3.34	1.52
1960	2.37	3.67	3.41	1.56
1961	2.28	3.53	3.25	1.52
1962	2.21	3.49	3.21	1.46
1963	2.22	3.50	3.24	1.47
1964	2.24	3.53	3.24	1.47
1965	2.24	3.54	3.25	1.44
1966	2.24	3.56	3.27	N.A.

Sources: Based on data in Appendix Tables A-1 and A-2.

Appendix Table A-4
National Economic Trends in Real Terms, 1929-1966
(In Billions of 1958 Dollars)

	Total Gross National Product	Personal Consumption Expenditures	Disposable Personal Income	Total Corporate Sales
1929	203.6	139.6	150.6	267.1
1930	183.3	130.4	139.0	251.2
1931	169.2	126.1	133.7	232.7
1932	144.1	114.8	115.1	194.9
1933	141.5	112.8	112.2	202.8
1934	154.3	118.1	120.4	219.6
1935	169.6	125.5	131.8	233.9
1936	193.0	138.4	148.4	271.6
1937	203.3	143.1	153.1	274.3
1938	193.0	140.2	143.6	253.7
1939	200.4	148.2	155.9	287.6
1940	227.2	155.7	166.3	315.9
1941	263.7	165.4	190.3	370.2
1942	297.8	161.4	213.4	377.0
1943	337.2	165.8	222.8	414.6
1944	361.3	171.4	231.6	435.1
1945	355.4	183.0	229.7	415.1
1946	312.6	203.5	227.0	411.7
1947	309.9	206.3	218.0	429.9
1948	323.7	210.8	229.8	444.2
1949	324.1	216.5	230.8	444.8
1950	355.3	230.5	249.6	498.4
1951	383.4	233.8	255.7	507.2
1952	395.1	239.4	262.3	533.7
1953	412.8	250.8	275.4	567.0
1954	407.0	255.7	278.3	558.4
1955	438.0	274.2	296.7	645.9
1956	446.1	281.4	309.3	660.1
1957	452.5	288.2	315.8	681.3
1958	447.3	290.1	318.8	658.2
1959	475.9	307.3	333.0	737.9

Appendix Table A-4 (continued)

	Total Gross National Product	Personal Consumption Expenditures	Disposable Personal Income	Total Corporate Sales
1960	487.8	316.2	340.2	761.0
1961	497.3	322.6	350.7	781.6
1962	529.8	338.4	367.3	847.4
1963	551.0	353.3	381.3	893.5
1964	580.0	373.8	406.5	962.9
1965	614.4	396.2	430.8	1,035.1
1966	641.7	415.5	451.5	N.A.

Sources: Economic Report of the President, January 1967, Washington, D.C., pp. 214, 232; U.S. Department of Commerce, Office of Business Economics, *National Income,* 1954 Edition, Washington, D.C., 1954, pp. 204-205; *U.S. Income and Output,* Washington, D.C., 1958, p. 215; *Survey of Current Business,* July 1962, p. 27, July 1964 p. 28, and July 1966, p. 11, 18, 35.

Note: Gross national product, personal consumption expenditures, disposable personal income data are as reported; corporate sales were deflated by all commodities of the wholesale price index.

Appendix Table A-5
Relationship between Advertising Expenditures and Economic Aggregates

1	2	3	4	5
Years	Relation of Advertising Expenditures to	Increase in Advertising Expenditures Per Dollar Increase in Economic Aggregate (cents)	Average Increase in Ratio of Advertising to Economic Aggregate Per $100 Billion Increase in Economic Aggregate* (percentage points)	Coefficient of Determination
1935-65	Total Gross National Product	20.39 (.07)	0.086	.977
1935-65	Personal Consumption Expenditures	3.80 (.08)	0.025	.987
1935-65	Disposable Personal Income	3.55 (0.10)	0.245	.978
1935-65	Total Corporate Sales	1.52	0.017	.987

Appendix Table A-5 (continued)

1	2	3	4	5
Years	Relation of Advertising Expenditures to	Increase in Advertising Expenditures Per Dollar Increase in Economic Aggregate (cents)	Average Increase in Ratio of Advertising to Economic Aggregate Per $100 Billion Increase in Economic Aggregate* (percentage points)	Coefficient of Determination
1935-40 1946-49 & 1954-65	Total Gross National Product	2.31 (.05)	0.026	.990
1935-40, 1946-49 & 1954-65	Personal Consumption Expenditures	3.75 (.09)	0.153	.987
1935-40, 1946-49 & 1954-65	Disposable Personal Income	3.43 (.09)	0.120	.987
1935-40 1946-49 & 1954-65	Total Corporate Sales	1.49 (.03)	-0.001	.991

*The ratio of advertising expenditure (y) to the economic aggregate (x) is $r = y/x$ or $r = \dfrac{a + bx}{x} = \dfrac{a}{x} + b$ where a is the intercept and b is the slope. The change in the ratio r per unit change in x is $\dfrac{-a}{x^2}$ and when x is given its average value we arrive at the average increase in the ratio r (column 4).

Appendix Table A-6
Advertising Expenditures Data: Printers' Ink, Internal Revenue Service and Advertising Age, by Years, 1945 to 1962

	Printers' Ink	IRS (millions)	Advertising Age
1945	$2,875	$1,923	N.A.
1946	3,364	2,408	N.A.
1947	4,264	3,032	4,241
1948	4,864	3,466	4,907
1949	5,202	3,773	5,331
1950	5,710	4,097	5,864
1951	6,426	4,553	6,497
1952	7,156	5,027	7,161
1953	7,755	5,481	7,784
1954	8,164	5,770	8,080
1955	9,194	6,602	8,997
1956	9,905	7,062	9,674
1957	10,311	7,666	10,313
1958	10,302	7,875	10,414
1959	11,255	8,747	11,358
1960	11,932	9,291	11,900
1961	11,845	9,563	12,048
1962	12,381	10,391	12,919

Note: IRS data are not available prior to 1945.

N.A. — not available

Source: U.S. Treasury Department, Internal Revenue Service, *Statistics of Income, Corporation Income Tax Returns,* 1945 to 1962-63, passim; *Printers' Ink, Guide to Marketing for 1963,* August 31, 1962, pp. 384-85 and January 31, 1964, p. 5, *Advertising Age,* June 13, 1966, p. 82.

Appendix Table A-7
Percent Distribution of Advertising Expenditures by Media, Selected Years, 1935-1966

Year	Magazines	News-papers	Radio	Tele-vision	Direct Mail	Out-door	Farm Publi-cations	Busi-ness Papers	Miscel-laneous	Total
1935	8.0	45.1	6.7	-	16.7	1.8	0.2	3.0	18.5	100.0
1940	9.5	39.0	10.3	-	16.0	2.2	0.3	3.6	19.1	100.0
1945	12.7	32.1	14.8	-	10.1	2.5	0.3	7.1	20.4	100.0
1950	9.0	36.3	10.6	3.0	14.1	2.5	0.4	4.4	19.7	100.0
1955	7.9	33.6	5.9	11.1	14.1	2.1	0.4	4.9	20.0	100.0
1960	7.9	31.1	5.8	13.3	15.3	1.7	0.3	5.1	19.5	100.0
1965	7.9	29.2	6.0	16.5	15.2	1.2	0.2	4.4	19.4	100.0
1966	7.8	29.5	6.1	16.7	14.8	1.1	0.2	4.3	19.5	100.0

Source: Derived from Appendix Table A-1.

Appendix Table A-8
Advertising Expenditures, Eight Media, 1940, 1950, and 1965

	1940	1950	1965	Increase 1940-65	1950-65
			(millions)		
Newspaper	$815	$2,076	$4,457	$3,642	$2,381
Television	0	171	2,515	2,515	2,344
Direct mail	334	803	2,324	1,990	1,521
Magazines	198	515	1,199	1,001	684
Radio	216	605	917	701	312
Business papers	76	251	671	595	420
Outdoor	45	143	180	135	37
Farm publications	7	21	34	27	13
Total Media	1,691	4,585	12,297	10,606	7,712

Source: Derived from Appendix Table A-1.

Appendix B

Implicit Advertising Cost Index and the Trend of Real Advertising Media Expenditures

The significance of the dollar expenditures for advertising is influenced by the costs for advertising which are a composite of the dollars paid per line, per page, or per hour *and* the exposure of the message. To determine the increases in the real volume of advertising in contrast to the dollar totals which have been affected by price inflation, it is necessary to eliminate the price factor.

Two types of cost information are available: 1] an index of the actual cost per page, per line, or per hour and 2] an index which adjusts the actual cost data for the exposure of the advertising. The two types may be illustrated by magazines. The costs per page, circulation, and cost per thousand circulation for magazines have been as follows since 1960.[1]

	Magazine Cost Per Page	Circulation	Cost Per Thousand Circulation
	(1960 = 100)		
1961	110	105	105
1962	118	111	107
1963	122	115	106
1964	124	118	105
1965	127	121	105

1 *Printers' Ink,* January 14, 1966, p. 12.

Between 1960 and 1965, the average cost for advertising per black and white page increased by 27%. However, the exposure as measured by circulation increased by 21%. In other words, most of the increase in the cost per page was offset by a greater exposure of the advertising message. By dividing the magazine cost index by the circulation index, the price of the advertising or the increase in the cost per thousand circulation is derived.

There is general agreement that "Since the basic function of an advertising medium is that of a carrier of messages to people, the cost-per-thousand delivered messages give us an accurate yardstick by which to measure the trend of true media costs."[2] This is the meaningful measure of the price of advertising, since it takes into account the number of readers or viewers who may see the advertising. In the following discussion, the cost for media advertising will be used in this sense.

However, it must be recognized that data per thousand for the printed media probably are more meaningful than those for radio and television. The use of number of homes probably results in some overstatement of the exposure obtained through TV and hence understates the cost per exposure. Thus, for example, if no one is at home the advertising message over TV or radio is forever lost to that family. On the other hand, the magazine and the newspaper can be read at one's convenience, and hence there is not the void that is possible for radio and TV. This is not intended to suggest that every reader reads or studies every advertisement in the printed media. But it does mean there is greater opportunity to do so and that, therefore, the data for those media probably are more satisfactory. Hours of usage for radio and TV are not subject to the same criticism. They are more comparable to the circulation data for the printed media.

2 Lyndon O. Brown, "A New Look At Advertising Costs," an Address Before the Association of National Advertisers, Spring Meeting, May 21-22, 1962, p. 6. See also O. J. Firestone, *Broadcast Advertising in Canada.* University of Ottawa Press, Ottawa, Canada, 1966, pp. 106-10.

Because of limitations in these data, potential exposure cost comparisons among media generally are not regarded as too significant.

Television Costs

There is no general agreement concerning the best method by which to measure the cost of television; hence varying estimates are available. *Printers' Ink* index of television usage is determined by multiplying the number of television homes in the country by the estimated average number of hours of viewing per home per day. Separate data are reported by *Printers' Ink* for network and for spot television. Reported declines in their indexes for the cost of TV have been due to the much larger increase in usage than in the cost of time, as the following data for *network* television show.[3]

Years	Network Time and Talent Cost Index	Index of Television Usage (1960 = 100)	Index of Cost Per Million Hours of Usage
1961	103	104	99
1962	106	108	98
1963	110	112	98
1964	114	120	95
1965	119	125	94

Indexes prepared by other sources show different trends for television costs than the *Printers' Ink* data. For example, the A. C. Nielsen index of cost of *prime time network television per thousand households* increased by 23% between 1960 and 1965 and the cost of *fringe time spot television* increased by 15.7%. Unlike the *Printers' Ink* data, the estimates make no allowance for hours of usage, and those for network television do not cover program costs. Moreover, this index covers only *prime* network time (7:30 p.m. to 11 p.m.) while the *Printers' Ink* data cover *all* network time. Since the cost of prime evening time has risen much more than other television costs, the former index overstates the increase in average television costs.

3 *Printers' Ink,* January 14, 1966, p. 12.

Ted Bates & Co. Media Program Department prepares estimates of cost per thousand audience tuned in for four categories of television time. The changes between 1960 and 1965 were as follows:[4]

		% Change
TV evening	(7:30 p.m. to 11 p.m.)	+ 6
TV day	(10 a.m. to 5 p.m.)	– 31
TV fringe spot	(5 p.m. to 7:30 p.m.)	
	(11 p.m. to 1 a.m.)	+ 17
TV day spot	(10 a.m. to 5 p.m.)	+ 1

The Bates data cover day and prime time network programs separately, the Nielsen data prime time network, and *Printers' Ink* all television network. The Bates data reflect the size of the audience and *Printers' Ink* the hours of usage, while A. C. Nielsen data are based on the number of television homes. Thus, the marked differences in trends recorded by these indexes reflect largely the fact that they are not measuring the same time periods or the same exposure.

It is not within the scope of this study to attempt to resolve this intricate problem of measurement. The *Printers' Ink* data are used in the following estimates. It must be recognized, however, that they may overstate the decline in television costs per exposure and hence result in some understatement of the rise in average media costs; the result would be some overstatement of the rise in real advertising expenditures. However, the margin of error, if any, is probably not great, because TV network costs in 1965 accounted for $1,246 million or only 14.0% and spot TV for $866 million or only 9.7% of the $8.9 billion of media advertising expenditures for which cost data were available.[5]

4 *Television Magazine,* November 1966, p. 37.

5 For example, if instead of the decline of 11% for television costs recorded by the *Printers' Ink* index between 1957-59 and 1965, there was no change, the implicit cost index would have been 109.4 for 1965 instead of 107.4. (See Appendix Table B-3.) If television costs had risen by 10% instead of the reported 11% decline, the index would be 110.9. Thus, it seems clear that the use of alternate estimates of the changes in television costs would have only a small effect upon long-term changes in the implicit cost index.

Implicit Advertising Cost Index

Advertising cost indexes have been published by *Printers' Ink* for 1946 and from 1950 to 1965 for the various media, except local radio, local television, farm publications, and direct mail. (See Appendix Table B-1.) The diverse changes in these cost indexes between 1955 and 1965 and 1960 and 1965 are shown in Chart B-1. Of the $12.2 billion spent for media advertising in 1965, these cost or rate data are available for $8.9 billion or 72% of the total.

To determine the effect of price increases on the total media advertising bill, the indexes of costs have been converted to a 1957-59 base as 100. This is the base period used for most government statistics, including the wholesale price index and the retail price index. The total expenditures for each medium have been divided by the appropriate price indexes thus derived. For example, magazine advertising expenditures were divided by the rate per thousand

CHART B-1

Advertising Cost Changes per Unit of Exposure, 1955-1965 and 1960-1965
(in percent)

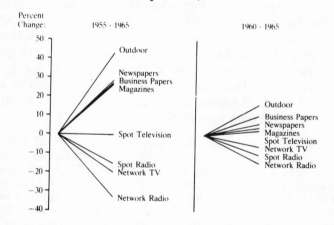

circulation for magazines, etc. The resulting deflated data for each of 8 categories of media expenditures are shown in Appendix Table B-2. These deflated totals were then aggregated. By dividing the total money expenditures for the eight media by this aggregate, an implicit advertising cost index is obtained. Appendix Table B-3 shows both aggregates and the resulting implicit cost index. The trends of the implicit cost index are compared with those for several media in Chart B-2.

To check the implicit cost index obtained, a weighted cost index was also calculated. The total volume of advertising expenditures for each of the eight media was calculated for the years 1957 to 1959. The proportion of the total for all eight media accounted for by each one was then deter-

CHART B-2

Advertising Cost Indexes by Media and Implicit Advertising Cost Index, 1946, 1950-65

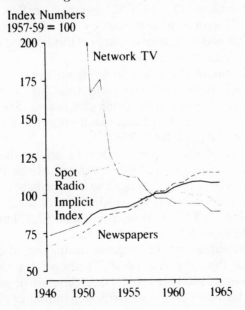

mined. The weights derived for each category are shown below.

	Percent of Total
Newspapers	52.9
Magazines	12.9
TV—network	11.8
TV—spot	6.5
Radio—network	0.9
Radio—spot	3.1
Business papers	8.8
Outdoor advertising	3.1
Total	100.0

The cost indexes for each year were combined on the basis of these constant weights as is done by the U.S. Bureau of Labor Statistics for its price indexes. The index obtained is compared with the implicit index in Appendix Table B-4 and Chart B-3. Although there were marked differences between the two indexes in 1951 and 1952, in the other years they were similar. The 1951-52 disparities reflect the sharp decline in TV costs during the early years of this new medium. This decline had a greater impact on the implicit index than on the weighted price index.

To eliminate the price factor from the dollar expenditures for all media advertising, the total for each year was divided by the implicit advertising cost index. (See Appendix Table B-2). The results of this calculation are shown in the last column of Appendix Table B-3.

The use of the implicit index to adjust the unpriced areas may result in some overstatement of the increase in real advertising expenditures. The media expenditures for which cost indexes were not available were local radio $569 million, local TV $411 million, direct mail $2,324 million, and farm publications $34 million.

It is probable that the increase in the cost of direct mail was greater than the rise of 46.7% shown for the implicit index between 1946 and 1965. Thus, the cost of postage has increased between 50% and 167% depending upon the type of postage used.[6] There also have been large increases in

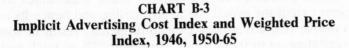

CHART B-3
Implicit Advertising Cost Index and Weighted Price Index, 1946, 1950-65

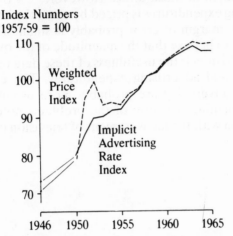

the cost of paper,[7] of printing[8] and of wages[9] during the post-World War II period. While the price of direct mail probably rose more than the implicit index, the cost of local radio and

6 For example, rates for third-class mail increased from 1½ cents for the first 2 ounces per single piece in 1946 to 4 cents in January 1963 or by 167%, while the bulk rate increased from 12 cents per pound to 18 cents per pound or by 50%. For books and catalogues the increase was from 8 cents a pound to 12 cents a pound or by 50%. Most of the third-class mail probably qualifies for the bulk rate, so that the average rise from 1946 to 1965 has been somewhat in excess of 50%.

7 The BLS wholesale price of paper increased by 89% between 1946 and 1965.

8 Average hourly earnings for printing and publishing rose by 107% between 1947 and 1965 (data are available only since 1947).

9 Data are not available for wage costs of direct mail. Weekly earnings in all manufacturing industries increased 148% between 1946 and 1965. In light of the enormous increase in the level of wages in the economy in the postwar years, labor costs also have undoubtedly risen sharply for direct mail.

local TV probably increased less.

It is probable that the implicit index understates to a minor extent the actual rise in advertising and hence its use to derive real advertising expenditures may result in some overstatement in those totals. However, 72% of total media advertising expenditures is priced by using the implicit index; hence any margin of error probably is small. Thus, there is no reason to believe that the magnitude of the overstatement is such as to impair the usefulness of these data to show broad trends in real advertising expenditures. The estimates for total real advertising are probably more useful than those for each medium because of the problems noted earlier in connection with the measurement of television costs.

Appendix Table B-1

Advertising Cost Indexes, by Media, 1940-1946, 1950-1965
(1957-59 = 100)

	Magazines (per 1000 circulation)	Newspapers (per million lines)	Television Network (per million homes per hour)	Television Spot	Radio Network	Radio Spot	Business Papers (per 1000 circulation)	Outdoor Advertising (per 1000 vehicle registrations)
1940	68	67	NA	NA	NA	NA	NA	98
1941	66	66	NA	NA	NA	NA	NA	92
1942	64	64	NA	NA	NA	NA	NA	98
1943	65	64	NA	NA	NA	NA	NA	103
1944	67	60	NA	NA	NA	NA	NA	107
1945	67	63	NA	NA	NA	NA	NA	109
1946	66	65	NA	NA	248	NA	NA	105
1950	75	75	278	167	208	112	84	91
1951	78	79	167	120	208	116	81	87
1952	83	83	175	133	171	117	85	93
1953	85	86	127	103	135	119	85	89
1954	88	88	114	105	138	121	87	89
1955	89	89	111	103	115	109	88	88
1956	91	92	111	115	110	97	96	90
1957	94	96	103	102	110	98	100	95
1958	102	102	97	100	94	101	98	99
1959	104	102	97	100	96	101	102	105
1960	107	107	94	100	90	102	101	107
1961	112	109	94	102	88	101	104	112
1962	114	112	94	100	83	99	105	114
1963	114	114	94	103	81	99	107	118
1964	112	114	89	102	79	97	110	121
1965	112	114	89	103	77	92	112	125

Sources: 1946 and 1950 to 1965, *Printers Ink*, June 7, 1957, pp. 25, 62, 64, 67, 68; October 30, 1959, Section One, pp. 341, 343-45; January 10, 1964, pp. 7-8; January 8, 1965, pp. 5, 6, 8; January 14, 1966, p. 12. Magazine Publishers Association and *Editor and Publisher* for 1940-45 data for magazines and newspapers respectively.

Notes: Data for 1947-49 are not available. Data for 1960-65 chained on to earlier years which may not be fully comparable. NA — Not available

Appendix Table B-2
Real Advertising Expenditures, by Media 1940-1946, 1950-1965 (in millions of 1957-59 dollars)

	Magazines (per 1000 circulation)	Newspapers (per million lines)	Television Network (per million homes per hour)	Television Spot	Radio Network	Radio Spot	Business Papers (per 1000 circulation)	Outdoor Advertising (per 1000 vehicle registrations)
1940	291	1,216	NA	NA	NA	NA	NA	46
1941	324	1,279	NA	NA	NA	NA	NA	58
1942	311	1,247	NA	NA	NA	NA	NA	45
1943	423	1,406	NA	NA	NA	NA	NA	41
1944	484	1,480	NA	NA	NA	NA	NA	52
1945	545	1,462	NA	NA	NA	NA	NA	66
1946	647	1,782	NA	NA	81	NA	251	82
1950	687	2,768	31	19	94	121	310	157
1951	736	2,858	108	58	87	119	344	171
1952	742	2,980	146	71	95	121	429	174
1953	785	3,076	252	142	104	123	465	198
1954	759	3,063	370	197	83	112	469	210
1955	819	3,470	486	252	73	123	507	218
1956	874	3,517	563	286	55	166	517	223
1957	866	3,420	650	345	58	191	568	209
1958	752	3,130	731	397	62	188	536	195
1959	833	3,476	763	486	46	204	558	184
1960	879	3,461	833	527	48	218	603	190
1961	825	3,324	944	523	49	216	556	161
1962	854	3,287	1,038	611	55	231	569	150
1963	907	3,337	1,090	659	69	240	575	145
1964	989	3,639	1,272	765	75	259	566	145
1965	1,071	3,910	1,400	841	77	285	599	144

Note: Derived by dividing actual dollar advertising expenditures in Appendix Table A-1 by the corresponding annual indexes for costs of each medium in Appendix Table B-1.

Appendix Table B-3

Estimated Total Real Media Advertising Expenditures, 1946, 1950-1966

	1 Advertising In 8 Media Actual Expenditures (millions)	2 Advertising In 8 Media Expenditures In 1957-59 dollars	3 Implicit Cost Index (1 ÷ 2)	4 All Media Advertising † Actual Expenditures	5 All Media Advertising † Expenditures in 1957-59 dollars (millions)
1946	$2,082*	$2,843*	73.2	$2,684	$3,667
1950	3,317	4,187	80.2	4,585	5,717
1951	3,842	4,481	85.7	5,161	6,022
1952	4,270	4,758	89.7	5,747	6,407
1953	4,636	5,145	90.1	6,230	6,915
1954	4,836	5,263	91.9	6,560	7,138
1955	5,473	5,948	92.0	7,358	7,998
1956	5,904	6,201	95.2	7,957	8,358
1957	6,137	6,307	97.3	8,252	8,481
1958	6,031	5,990	100.7	8,272	8,214
1959	6,650	6,550	101.5	9,049	8,915
1960	7,031	6,759	104.0	9,604	9,235
1961	6,986	6,598	105.9	9,524	8,993
1962	7,284	6,795	107.2	10,022	9,349
1963	7,622	7,022	108.5	10,584	9,756
1964	8,276	7,710	107.3	11,405	10,629
1965	8,940	8,327	107.4	12,278	11,432

* Excludes network and spot television and spot radio.
† Includes local radio, local TV, direct mail, and farm publications in addition to the eight media shown in Appendix Tables B-1 and B-2.

Appendix Table B-4
Implicit Advertising Cost Index and Weighted Cost Index for Advertising, 1946, 1950-1965

	Implicit Index	Weighted Price Index (1957-59 = 100)
1946	73.2	70.8
1950	80.2	79.3
1951	85.7	95.1
1952	89.7	99.4
1953	90.1	93.4
1954	91.9	93.8
1955	92.0	93.2
1956	95.2	96.2
1957	97.3	97.4
1958	100.7	100.7
1959	101.5	101.6
1960	104.0	104.2
1961	105.9	106.4
1962	107.2	108.0
1963	108.5	109.7
1964	107.3	109.0
1965	107.4	109.2

Note: Television data not included in deriving indexes for 1946 and 1950.

Appendix C

Advertising-Sales Ratios
and
Changes in Prices

To determine the relationship between advertising and changes in prices, a study has been made of the experience during the post-World War II period. Despite some limitations, the best available measure of the intensity of advertising is the ratio of advertising expenditures to sales.

The Internal Revenue Service Source Book contains the most detailed breakdown available for sales and advertising expenditures by industries. Each year *Advertising Age* derives from these data ratios of advertising to sales for more than 270 industries. From this tabulation, the consumer goods industries were selected and where possible these advertising-sales ratios were matched against changes in wholesale and retail prices published by the U.S. Bureau of Labor Statistics.

Since the IRS data are published several years late, the most recent relationships available in 1966 were for the fiscal year 1962-63; this actually covers the calendar year 1962 for the vast majority of companies. Although there are small year-to-year changes in an industry's advertising-sales ratio, a review of the data for earlier years indicates that industries tend to follow fairly consistent advertising spending patterns over time.

Several limitations of advertising-sales ratios should be noted. First, the data cover a composite of many diverse products because of the conglomerate nature of many companies. The advertising-sales ratios undoubtedly are higher or lower for many product lines than indicated by these composite data for industries. Secondly, as noted in Appendix A, the Internal Revenue Service reports data only for corporations. The inclusion of partnerships and individual proprietorships probably would change the reported ratios to a small extent. Third, the ratios are based on manufacturing industries alone. There is also a considerable amount of advertising by retailers, although it varies from the pattern for manufacturers.

Price data are not available for every industry for which advertising-sales ratios were obtained, and often it is difficult to match up BLS and IRS data. BLS has not priced all products for the entire postwar period. This is particularly true of retail prices for which the BLS pricing program was significantly expanded in 1964. Appendix Table C-1 lists the 30 products

CHART C-1

Advertising Outlays per Dollar of Sales, 1962, and Percent Change in Wholesale Prices for Selected Products, 1957-59 to June 1966

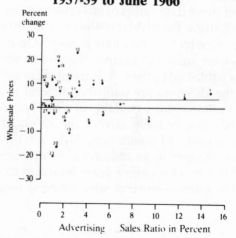

or product groups for which wholesale prices are reported by BLS for the postwar years. Data were available for the entire period for 29 groups, while for one group, motorcycles and bicycles, data are available only for the period since 1957-59.

Appendix Table C-2 lists 22 products for which retail prices were available; for 16 products comparisons could be made with 1947 while for an additional 6 they can be made only since 1957-59. In the footnotes to the tables, the differences between the price data and the advertising-sales ratio categories are described.

The price increase from 1947 to 1965 was calculated to

CHART C-2
Advertising Outlays per Dollar of Sales, 1962, and Percent Change in Retail Prices for Selected Products, 1947 to 1965

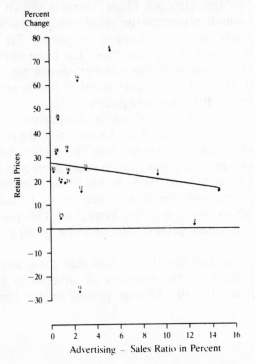

show long-term trends; for the shorter period the changes from 1957-59 to June 1966 were determined. The tables also show the relative weights of each of these commodity groups in the WPI in December 1962 and the weights in the CPI in December 1963.

To portray the relationships between advertising intensity and price changes, scatter charts have been prepared. Chart V-3 in the text shows the relationship between advertising-sales ratios and changes in wholesale prices between 1947 and 1965. Chart C-1 shows the relationship for the 1957-59-June 1966 period. Charts C-2 and C-3 show similar scatters for retail prices.

The coefficient of correlation and the coefficient of determination were calculated and the mathematical relationship between the two sets of data were determined for each of the 4 charts. Appendix Table C-3 shows these mathematical relationships. On each chart, there is shown a line of regression which expresses the relationship between advertising intensity and the changes in prices. To facilitate identification, each dot on the chart has been numbered so that it corresponds with the number shown on Appendix Tables C-1 and C-2. The same number has been used for retail prices and for wholesale prices.

Although the number of usable comparisons is not very large, the data include most of the intensive users of advertising. Four of the five groups with the highest advertising to sales ratios recorded less than average increases in wholesale prices from 1947 to 1965. At the other extreme, two of the five groups with the lowest advertising to sales ratios recorded above-average price increases. The pattern was the same for retail prices, although the groups were not identical.

The tables and the charts show that there has been no correlation between the intensity of advertising and price changes either for the 18-year period or for the shorter period.

CHART C-3

Advertising Outlays per Dollar of Sales, 1962, and Percent Change in Retail Prices for Selected Products, 1957-59 to June 1966

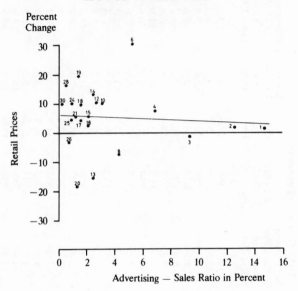

Appendix Table C-1
Advertising-Sales Ratio, 1962, and Changes
in Wholesale Prices, Selected Periods,
1947 to 1966 (Percent)

		Advertising Outlays Per Dollar of Sales, 1962	Weights in WPI, Dec. 1962	1947 to 1965	Changes in Wholesale Prices		
					1957-59 to 1965	1957-59 to Dec. 1965	1957-59 to June 1966
1	Toilet preparations	14.72	.355	21.6	4.2	4.8	6.6
2	Soap, detergents	12.55	.563	5.7	4.5	4.4	4.2
3	Drugs1	9.39*	.859	−16.2	−5.6	−5.4	−5.5
4	Beer and malt	6.89	.674	38.0	0.9	1.6	1.4
5	Clocks and watches	5.45	.126	10.4	−4.2	−4.2	−3.0
6	Tobacco2	5.28	.752	48.4	5.8	5.6	10.0
7	Wines, brandy	4.58	.103	−2.8	11.4	11.6	9.7
8	Confectionery3	4.22	.099	20.7	−0.7	−6.6	−6.6
9	Cutlery, hand tools, hardware	3.28	.593	77.4	5.9	7.0	9.5
10	Grain-mill products4	3.18	.449	3.1	13.3	15.3	22.8
11	Photographic equipment	3.11	.142	28.8	7.3	7.4	6.8
12	Canning5	2.72	1.023	9.3	2.1	5.1	4.8
13	Appliances	2.48	.953	−3.6	−10.8	−11.2	−10.6
14	Bakery6	2.48	1.397	48.2	7.9	10.4	12.4
15	Distilled liquor	2.18	.269	−3.3	−2.8	−2.8	−2.8
16	Tires and tubes	2.09	.533	34.7	−10.0	−8.9	−5.6
17	Paints and varnish7	1.65	.312	36.5	5.4	5.9	6.8
18	Dairy products8	1.57	2.594	27.5	8.5	11.3	17.0
19	Footwear	1.43	.786	43.2	10.7	13.8	19.1
20	Radio and television9	1.37	.454	−17.0	−14.8	−11.5	−16.5
21	Household furniture	1.25	.957	37.5	6.2	6.7	8.9
22	Floor coverings	1.18	.228	34.9	−5.6	−6.0	−2.9
23	Knit goods	1.07	.082	−32.9	−8.4	−16.5	−20.4

Appendix Table C-1 (continued)

		Advertising Outlays Per Dollar of Sales, 1962	Weights in WPI, Dec. 1962	Changes in Wholesale Prices			
				1947 to 1965	1957-59 to 1965	1957-59 to Dec. 1965	1957-59 to June 1966
24	Men's, youths' and boys' apparel	.97	1.182	11.6	8.7	10.1	11.3
25	Women's, misses and children's clothing	.96	1.499	0.4	2.2	2.6	2.7
26	Motor vehicles	.74	3.923	53.7	0.7	0.5	0.7
27	Motorcycles and bicycles 1C	.67	.072	NA	-4.3	-4.2	-2.9
28	Meats	.56	3.579	6.1	0.8	12.1	8.6
29	Petroleum refining11	.49	4.044	26.5	-4.1	-1.6	0.2
30	Sugar	.28	.383	24.0	11.0	12.8	11.0
	Total Wholesale Price Index			26.2	2.5	4.1	5.7

* 1961

Notes: The price data used are indicated by the following footnotes.

1 Drugs and pharmaceuticals
2 Cigarettes, non-filter tip, regular size
3 Candy bars: solid chocolate
4 Includes flour and flour base cake mix
5 Canned and frozen fruits and vegetables
6 Includes white bread, cookies and crackers
7 Prepared paint
8 Dairy products and ice cream
9 Television, radio receivers, and phonographs
10 Bicycles
11 Petroleum products, refined

Sources: Advertising outlays per dollar of sales are from the Internal Revenue Service and published in *Advertising Age*, July 6, 1964, p. 59 and June 7, 1965, pp. 101-2 and U. S. Department of Labor, Bureau of Labor Statistics.

209

Appendix Table C-2
Advertising-Sales Ratio, 1962 and Changes in Retail Prices, Selected Periods, 1947 to 1966 (Percent)

	Advertising Outlays Per Dollar of Sales, 1962	Weights in WPI, Dec. 1962	1947 to 1965	Changes in Retail Prices		
				1957-59 to 1965	1957-59 to Dec. 1965	1957-59 to June 1966
1 Toilet preparations	14.72	1.52	15.9	2.3	0.3	1.2
2 Soap, detergents	12.55	.26	1.2	0.4	0.9	1.4
3 Drugs1	9.39*	1.14	22.5	-1.9	-1.9	-1.4
4 Beer and malt	6.89	1.06	NA	5.4	6.2	7.5
6 Tobacco2	5.28	1.74	74.4	24.2	28.2	30.7
8 Confectionery3	4.22	.16	NA	4.9	-1.6	-7.3
10 Grain-mill products4	3.18	.20	24.9	9.5	9.1	10.4
12 Canning5	2.72	1.32	15.4	7.3	10.0	10.1
13 Appliances	2.48	1.36	-26.2	12.9	-15.2	-15.7
14 Bakery6	2.48	.86	63.7	10.0	10.7	13.2
15 Distilled liquor	2.18	.39	NA	5.3	5.8	5.7
16 Tires and tubes	2.09	.36	NA	-0.2	0.7	2.6
17 Paints and varnish7	1.65	.16	NA	3.3	3.6	4.7
18 Dairy products	1.57	2.80	23.3	5.0	6.1	9.6
19 Footwear	1.43	1.51	32.5	12.9	15.6	19.8
20 Radio and television	1.37	.81	NA	-14.2	-18.0	-18.6
21 Household furniture8	1.25	1.44	19.4	2.8	3.1	5.2
24 Men's, youths' and boys' apparel	.97	2.86	20.0	7.4	9.3	10.1
25 Women's, misses, and children's clothing	.96	4.08	4.5	3.1	4.3	4.7
26 Motor vehicles	.74	2.55	45.8	-1.0	-1.3	-3.2
28 Meats	.56	4.45	31.8	6.9	13.3	18.6
30 Sugar	.28	.16	24.0	8.1	8.6	9.9
All commodities			27.6	6.4	7.4	9.0

* 1961   Note: The price data used are indicated by the following footnotes: Sources: See Appendix Table C-1

1 Drugs and prescriptions   3 Chocolate bars   5 Processed fruits and vegetables   7 Exterior house paint
2 Non-filter tip, regular size   4 Flour   6 White bread and cookies   8 Furniture and bedding

Appendix Table C-3
Relationship Between Advertising-Sales Ratio, 1962, and Changes in Retail and Wholesale Prices, Selected Periods, 1947-1966

Period	Number of Industries	R	R^2	Equation
Wholesale Prices				
1947-65	29	$-.0943$	.0089	$Y = 21.933 - 0.648(X)$
				(1.317)
1957-59-June 1966	30	.0123	.0002	$Y = 3.143 + 0.034(X)$
				(0.531)
Retail Prices				
1947-65	16	$-.1464$	.0214	$Y = 27.488 - 0.771(x)$
				(1.392)
1957-59-June 1966	22	$-.0970$	.0094	$Y = 6.291 - 0.268(x)$
				(0.616)

As the standard errors of the slope of these straight-line equations (shown in parenthesis) more than equal the magnitude of the slopes, no significance can be attached to the lines of regression as determined in the above analysis.

Sources: Derived from data in Appendix Tables C-1 and C-2

Appendix D

Advertising and Profit Rates

Each year *Advertising Age*[1] publishes a list of 125 companies with the largest dollar expenditures for advertising. As part of this tabulation, the domestic sales for these companies and their advertising expenditures as a percentage of these sales are reported. Although these companies have the largest dollar expenditures, the degree of intensity of advertising—as measured by the advertising to sales ratio—varies widely among them. The return on invested capital[2] has been obtained for most of these companies in order to determine the relationship between earnings and intensity of advertising. This study has been made both for 1964 and 1965. Six of the 125 companies are privately owned, while five are subsidiaries of foreign corporations, so that profits data could be obtained for only 114 companies, of which nine were nonmanufacturing, in 1964;[3] for 1965 data were

[1] *Advertising Age,* August 30, 1965, p 38 and August 29, 1966, p 44.
[2] Data for profits and invested capital were obtained from *Fortune,* July 1965 and July 1966 and *Moody's Industrials,* 1965 and 1966.
[3] The 9 nonmanufacturing companies were American Telephone and Telegraph, Sears Roebuck, Columbia Broadcasting, and six airline companies.

available for 111 companies.

Although the company data provide a more satisfactory basis for study than either industry data or IRS data, there are several limitations that should be noted in connection with this study:

1] The list is not intended to be a cross-section sample of American industry. It shows only the experience of the largest advertisers as measured by dollars. However, these companies do have widely varying ratios of advertising to sales. For the 102 *manufacturing* companies in the 1965 study, the average advertising to sales ratio was 2.50% as compared with 1.38% for all manufacturing corporations in 1962.[4] The frequency distribution is shown below:

Advertising-Sales Ratio (percent)	No. of Companies 1964	1965
0 - 0.9	11	10
1.0 - 1.9	17	18
2.0 - 2.9	15	15
3.0 - 3.9	8	6
4.0 - 4.9	3	7
5.0 - 5.9	6	8
6.0 - 6.9	13	10
7.0 - 7.9	5	6
8.0 - 8.9	4	2
9.0 - 9.9	3	2
10.0 -10.9	4	5
11.0 -11.9	3	0
12.0 -12.9	1	5
13.0 -13.9	1	0
14.0 -14.9	0	0
15.0 -15.9	5	7
20.0 -24.9	8	5
25.0 and over	7	5
Total	114	111

43 companies or approximately two-fifths (38.7%) of the 1965 sample had advertising ratios of less than 3%, while 37 companies or one-third had ratios of 7% or higher. The

4 In 1964, the advertising-sales ratio averaged 2.66% for 105 manufacturing companies.

distribution was similar in 1964 with 37.7% below 3% and 37% with 7% or higher. Clearly, this group of advertisers is heavily weighted by companies which have above-average advertising-sales ratios.

2] The advertising-sales ratios are based upon domestic sales, while the profit experience reflects worldwide results of these companies where they also operate outside the U.S. Disparities in earnings on foreign business as compared with domestic business could influence the results shown. In addition, comparisons between companies in the same industry may be affected by varying proportions of sales to government agencies and to other business firms.

3] The use of relationships for a single year may be distorted, either because the ratio of advertising may be unusually high or low for some companies as a result of temporary factors or because the profit experience is affected by special factors such as the timing of wage and price changes, the timing of introduction of new products, and/or sudden expansions or falling off in demand. Moreover, the profit results in a single year may reflect the cumulative impact of advertising expenditures over several years, particularly where they have been increasing or decreasing fairly steadily. The experience in years like 1964 and 1965 may not be representative for profits because these were boom years after 3 years of steady expansion.

4] The total invested capital of these companies may be understated because of the significant price inflation during the past quarter of a century and the fact that these companies fail to reflect goodwill on their balance sheets. The latter factor may be particularly important for heavy advertisers. As a result, when reported profits are related to understated asset values, the net effect must be to inflate the reported return on net assets.

5] Sales data include the taxes paid by each company. In some industries such as distilled spirits and cigarettes these taxes are a significant proportion of total sales.

1964 Study

Using a straight-line regression model, the following equation was determined:

$$Y = 11.854 + .240(x)$$
$$(.068)$$

where Y = return on invested capital   (Net profits divided by invested capital and expressed as a percent)

X = advertising-sales relationship (*Advertising Age* ratio in percent)

As the coefficient of the X value (.240) is more than 3 times its standard error (.068), there is a relationship between the two variables. However, the coefficient of correlation (r) is only .315 and the coefficient of determination (r^2), which shows the direct relationship between the variables, is only .099. Thus, the relative level of advertising was associated with less than 10% of the difference in profit rates. There is considerable dispersion about the trend line as is shown in Chart D-1.

1965 Study

Using a straight-line regression model, the following equation was determined:

$$Y = 12.593 + .278(x)$$
$$(.072)$$

As the coefficient of the X value (.278) is more than 3 times its standard error (.072), there is a relationship between the two variables. However, the coefficient of correlation (r) is only .345 and the coefficient of determination (r^2) is only .119. Thus, the relative level of advertising was associated with about 12% of the difference in profit rates. There is considerable dispersion about the trend line as is shown in Chart VI-1 in the text.

The relationships in 1965 were substantially the same as those derived for 1964.

CHART D-1
Advertising Expenditures as a Percent of
Sales and Return on Invested Capital for
114 Large Advertisers, 1964

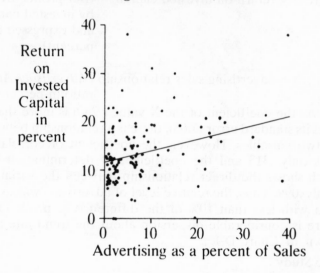

Appendix E

Statistical Tables

Appendix Table E-1
**Percent Relationship of Selected
Categories of Expenditures to Total
Personal Consumption Expenditures,
Selected Years, 1929 to 1965**

	Toilet Articles & Preparations		Cleaning & Polishing Preparations & Misc. Household Supplies & Paper Products		Drug Preparations and Sundries	
	Amount (millions)	Percent of PCE	Amount (millions)	Percent of PCE	Amount (millions)	Percent of PCE
1929	$591	0.77	$485	0.63	$604	0.78
1935	374	0.67	403	0.72	474	0.85
1940	507	0.72	544	0.77	635	0.90
1945	1,087	0.91	722	0.60	1,138	0.95
1950	1,354	0.71	1,768	0.93	1,719	0.90
1955	1,915	0.75	2,480	0.97	2,362	0.93
1960	2,970	0.91	3,397	1.04	3,607	1.11
1965	4,309	1.00	4,234	0.98	4,628	1.07

Source: *Survey of Current Business,* November 1965, pp. 20-23
and July 1966, p. 20.

Appendix Table E-2
Number of Firms by Pharmacological Field, 1953-1959

	1953	1954	1955	1956	1957	1958	1959
Hematinics	47	53	66	70	66	78	86
Diuretic	30	40	49	50	48	47	50
Penicillin and procaine	14	17	18	17	16	15	14
Penicillin and potassium	15	15	18	19	16	18	17
Vitamins and hormones	NA	NA	4	6	9	11	20
Ataractics	NA	NA	NA	3	14	27	31
Antidiarrheals	19	24	27	33	32	34	38
Antihemorroidals	25	23	24	24	27	28	30
Antihypertensive	25	34	41	48	50	54	56
Infant formulas, infant feeding and dietary supplements	23	26	32	32	33	32	32
Hormones (female) (estrogens)	26	34	44	45	42	51	54
Lipotropic	22	28	30	33	33	38	45
Fungicides	39	42	42	42	48	58	63
Antacid gastric	40	46	49	51	56	60	64
Vitamins (multiple)	45	50	57	61	66	75	80
Laxatives	28	38	40	39	43	49	52
Sulfonamides	20	27	30	37	33	37	41

N.A. not available

Source: Derived from James W. McKie, "An Economic Analysis of the Position of American Home Products Corporation in the Ethical Drug Industry," U.S. Senate Committee on the Judiciary, Subcommittee on Antitrust and Monopoly, *Hearings on Administered Prices*, Part 17, Washington, D.C., 1960, pp. 10026-10042.

Appendix Table E-3
Number of Products by Pharmacological Field, 1953-1959

	1953	1954	1955	1956	1957	1958	1959
Hematinics	171	237	298	341	309	348	381
Diuretic	70	90	99	119	104	98	109
Penicillin and procaine	57	73	66	70	67	38	55
Penicillin and potassium	58	67	77	80	77	66	56
Vitamins and hormones	NA	NA	5	9	15	23	32
Ataractics	NA	NA	NA	3	20	41	54
Antidiarrheals	34	42	63	65	65	71	76
Antihemorroidals	48	37	40	33	38	42	51
Antihypertensive	59	77	101	148	169	156	164
Infant formulas, infant feeding and dietary supplements	80	89	119	106	108	107	108
Hormones (female) (estrogens)	92	112	135	145	123	132	131
Lipotropic	35	46	46	55	60	65	87
Fungicides	70	81	77	91	110	126	121
Antacids gastric	80	108	119	138	142	147	157
Vitamins (multiple)	188	229	156	286	329	370	393
Laxatives	64	86	94	103	104	117	125
Sulfonamides	59	83	101	102	99	99	97

N.A. not available

Source: Derived from James W. McKie, "An Economic Analysis of the Position of American Home Products Corporation in the Ethical Drug Industry," U.S. Senate Committee on the Judiciary, Subcommittee on Antitrust and Monopoly, *Hearings on Administered Prices*, Part 17, Washington, D.C., 1960, pp. 10026-10042.

Appendix Table E-4
Advertising-Sales Ratio, 1957, and Four-Firm Concentration Ratio, 1958, 41 Consumer-Goods Industries

Name	Advertising-Sales Ratio, 1957		Four-Firm Concentration Ratio, 1958	
	Percent	Rank	Percent	Rank
Perfumes	14.723	1	29.0	30
Drugs	10.280	2	30.4	28
Soaps	7.938	3	63.0	7
Beer and malt	6.872	4	29.0	31
Clocks and watches	5.629	5	48.9	13
Other tobacco	5.429	6	77.0	3
Cereals	4.845	7	83.0	2
Wines	4.395	8	35.0	20
Hand tools	3.791	9	33.3	22
Confectionery	3.543	10	37.2	17
Appliances	3.296	11	43.0	16
Bakery	2.803	12	30.3	29
Books	2.702	13	16.0	36
Canning	2.658	14	31.0	26
Costume jewelry	2.498	15	12.0	38
Distilled liquor	2.408	16	60.0	8
Cigars	2.370	17	54.0	10
Jewelry (except costume)	2.202	18	32.4	23
Hats	2.124	19	63.2	6
Professional and scientific instruments	2.086	20	47.8	14
Carpets	2.052	21	51.4	11

Appendix Table E-4 (continued)

Name	Advertising-Sales Ratio, 1957		Four-Firm Concentration Ratio, 1958	
	Percent	Rank	Percent	Rank
Communication	2.034	22	44.3	15
Household and service	1.901	23	49.5	12
Dairy products	1.885	24	36.4	18
Tires and tubes	1.885	25	74.0	4
Grain-mill products	1.695	26	32.0	24
Furniture	1.451	27	18.4	35
Paints and varnish	1.450	28	35.4	19
Footwear	1.326	29	26.5	33
Women's clothing	1.263	30	9.6	39
Motorcycles and bicycles	1.078	31	58.0	9
Knit goods	1.075	32	18.9	34
Men's clothing	0.928	33	14.6	37
Furs	0.916	34	5.0	41
Motor vehicles	0.907	35	88.1*	1
Parts and accessories	0.700	36	33.3*	21
Meats	0.610	37	28.4	32
Petroleum refining	0.507	38	32.0	25
Millinery	0.326	39	6.0	40
Periodicals	0.304	40	31.0	27
Sugar	0.280	41	65.1	5

* 1954 concentration ratio, 1958 data not available.

Source: Derived from Lester G. Telser, "Advertising and Competition," *The Journal of Political Economy,* December 1964, p. 543.

Appendix Table E-5
Advertising-Sales Ratio, 1957, and Percent of Value of Shipments by Four Largest Firms, 1947 and 1958

	Advertising-Sales Ratio 1957	1947 Big Four Four Largest Firms	1947 Big Four % Point Change 1947-58	1958 Big Four Four Largest Firms	1958 Big Four % Point Change 1947-58	Four Largest in 1947 & 1958
Perfumes	14.72					
Toilet preparations		24	−8 & over	29	+8 & over	C
Drugs	10.28					
Pharmaceutical preparations		28	−8 & over	27	+3 to +7	C
Soaps	7.94					
Soap and Glycerin		79	+8 & over	90	+8 & over	A
Beer and Malt	6.87					
Beer and Ale		21	+3 to +7	28	+8 & over	C
Malt		49	−2 to +2	50	+8 & over	C
Clocks and Watches	5.63	41	+3 to +7	48	+8 & over	C
Other Tobacco	5.43					
Cigarettes		90	−8 & over	79	−8 & over	C
Hand Tools	3.79					
Hand saws and saw blades		66	−8 & over	49	−8 & over	C
Confectionery	3.54					
Confectionery products		17	−2 to +2	18	+3 to +7	C
Chocolate and Cocoa products		68	−2 to +2	71	+8 & over	C
Chewing gum		70	+8 & over	88	+8 & over	C

Appendix Table E-5 (continued)

	Advertising-Sales Ratio 1957	1947 Big Four		1958 Big Four		Four Largest in 1947 & 1958
		Four Largest Firms	% Point Change 1947-58	Four Largest Firms	% Point Change 1947-58	
Appliances						
Domestic Laundry Equipment	3.30	40	+8 & over	71	+8 & over	C
Vacuum Cleaners		61	+8 & over	70	+8 & over	C
Refrigeration Machinery (incl. Industrial)	2.80	39	−8 & over	39	−2 to +2	C
Bakery						
Bread and Crackers		72	−3 to −7	65	−3 to −7	A
Bread and related products		16	+3 to +7	22	+3 to −7	C
Books	2.70	18	−3 to −7	16	−2 to +2	C
Canned fruits and vegetables	2.66	27	−2 to +2	29	−2 to +2	B
Distilled Liquor	2.40	75	−8 & over	60	−8 & over	B
Cigars	2.37	41	+8 & over	54	+8 & over	B
Hats	2.12					
Fur Felt		47	+8 & over	65	+8 & over	C
Wool Felt		76	−8 & over	70	+8 & over	C
Straw		59	−8 & over	50	+8 & over	C
Professional & Scientific Instru.	2.07					
Photographic Equipment		61	+8 & over	65	+8 & over	B
Carpets	2.05					
Wool carpets		52	−8 & over	47	−2 to +2	C
Carpets & Rugs except wool		25	−8 & over	32	+8 & over	C

	Advertising-Sales Ratio 1957	1947 Big Four Four Largest Firms	1947 Big Four % Point Change 1947-58	1958 Big Four Four Largest Firms	1958 Big Four % Point Change 1947-58	Four Largest in 1947 & 1958
Communications	2.03					
Radios and Related Products	1.89	26	−2 to +2	27	+8 & over	C
Dairy Products						
Concentrated milk		50	−2 to +2	50	−2 to +2	A
Ice cream and ices		40	−8 & over	29	−2 to +2	C
Tires and tubes	1.89	77	−3 to −7	74	−3 to −7	B
Grain mill products	1.70					
Flour and meal		29	+8 & over	38	+8 & over	A
Rice milling		13	−3 to −7	43	+8 & over	C
Furniture	1.45					
Upholstered household furniture		14	−3 to −7	14	−2 to +2	C
Mattresses and bedsprings		36	−8 & over	28	−3 to −7	C
Paints and varnish	1.45	27	−2 to +2	25	−2 to +2	A
Footwear	1.33	28	−2 to +2	27	−2 to +2	B
Women's Clothing	1.26					
Dresses, unit price		3	−2 to +2	4	+3 to +7	C
Dresses, dozen price		13	−8 & over	12	+3 to +7	C
Corsets and allied garments		16	−2 to +2	29	+8 & over	C
Men's Clothing	0.93					
Men's and boys' suits & coats		9	−3 to −7	11	+3 to +7	C
Men's and boys' neckwear		20	−8 & over	17	+3 to +7	C
Work shorts		52	−8 & over	52	+8 & over	C

Appendix Table E-5 (continued)

	Advertising-Sales Ratio 1957	1947 Big Four		1958 Big Four		Four Largest in 1947 & 1958
		Four Largest Firms	% Point Change 1947-58	Four Largest Firms	% Point Change 1947-58	
Furs						
Fur goods	0.92	3	−2 to +2	5	+3 to +7	C
Furs, dressed and dyed	0.91	33	−8 & over	25	+8 & over	C
Motor vehicles						
Motor vehicles and parts		56	+8 & over	75	+8 & over	A
Millinery	0.33	7	−3 to −7	13	+3 to +7	C
Periodicals	0.30	34	−8 & over	31	−2 to +2	C
Sugar	0.28					
Raw cane sugar		36	−2 to +2	38	+8 & over	C
Cane sugar refining		70	−2 to +2	69	−2 to +2	A
Beet sugar		68	−3 to −7	64	−3 to −7	C

Note:

A The four largest companies had the same rank in 1947 and 1958.

B The same companies were the four largest in 1947 and 1958 but there was some shifting in rank.

C The four largest companies in 1947 were not all among the four largest in 1958.

Sources: Advertising costs: Lester G. Telser, "Advertising and Competition," *Journal of Political Economy*, December 1964, p. 543; *Concentration Ratios in Manufacturing Industry, 1958*, Report prepared by the Bureau of the Census for the Subcommittee on Antitrust and Monopoly of the Committee on the Judiciary, United States Senate, Part II, 87 Cong., 2nd sess., Washington, D.C., 1962, pp. 469-472.

Appendix Table E-6
Percent Relationship of Advertising to Total Compiled Receipts, July 1962-June 1963

	Total Compiled Receipts (in millions)	Advertising	Percent Relationship
All Industrial Groups	$949,305	$10,391	1.09
Agriculture, Forestry, and Fisheries	6,289	22	0.35
Total Mining	12,529	26	0.21
Metal Mining	1,938	*	0.02
Bituminous Coal and Lignite Mining	1,871	2	0.11
Crude Petroleum and Natural Gas	6,382	16	0.25
Mining and Quarrying of non-metallic minerals, and anthracite mining	2,338	7	0.30
Construction	41,065	96	0.24
Total Manufacturing	407,865	5,638	1.38
Beverage Industries	9,320	458	4.91
Food and Kindred Products	55,506	1,117	2.01
Tobacco Manufactures	5,444	286	5.25
Textile Mill Products	15,404	90	0.58
Apparel and Other Finished Products made from fabrics and similar materials	15,135	135	0.89
Lumber and Wood Products except Furniture	8,406	34	0.40
Furniture and fixtures	5,554	64	1.15

Appendix Table E-6 (continued)

	Total Compiled Receipts (in millions)	Advertising	Percent Relationship
Paper and Allied Products	13,290	105	0.79
Printing, Publishing, and Allied Industries	14,955	159	1.06
Chemicals and Allied Products	30,510	1,185	3.88
Petroleum Refining and Related Industries	41,060	198	0.48
Rubber and Miscellaneous Plastics Products	8,953	143	1,60
Leather and Leather Products	3,928	46	1.17
Stone, Clay, and Glass Products	11,260	87	0.77
Primary Metal Industries	28,724	110	0.38
Fabricated Metal Products(including ordnance), except Machinery and Transportation Equipment	23,517	201	0.85
Machinery, except electrical & transportation equip.	29,176	276	0.95
Electrical Machinery, Equipment, & Supplies	25,752	365	1.42
Transportation Equipment except Motor Vehicles	18,008	42	0.23
Motor Vehicles and Motor Vehicle Equipment	29,225	212	0.73
Professional, Scientific, and Controlling Instruments; Photographic & Optical Goods; Watches & Clocks	7,664	173	2.26
Other Manufacturing Industries	7,074	151	2.13
Total Transportation, Communication, Electric, Gas, and Sanitary Services	73,156	347	0.47
Transportation	33,205	169	0.51
Communication	17,488	111	0.63

227

Appendix Table E-6 (continued)

	Total Compiled Receipts (in millions)	Advertising	Percent Relationship
Electric and Gas Companies and Systems	21,889	66	0.30
Water Supply and Other Sanitary Services	574	1	0.17
Total Wholesale and Retail Trade	298,336	3,094	1.04
Total Wholesale Trade	144,810	812	0.56
Groceries and Related Products	29,133	88	0.30
Electrical Goods, Hardware, & Plumbing & Heating Equipment and Supplies	13,513	106	0.78
Other Wholesalers	102,165	619	0.61
Total Retail Trade	146,678	2,221	1.51
Food	35,549	467	1.31
General Merchandise	28,523	709	2.49
Apparel and Accessories	9,748	219	2.25
Furniture, Home Furnishings, & Equipment	6,656	193	2.90
Automotive Dealers and Gasoline Service Stations	35,802	303	0.85
Eating and Drinking Places	6,824	69	1.01
Building Materials, Hardware, & Farm Equipment	9,869	84	0.85
Other Retail Stores	13,706	177	1.29
Wholesale & Retail Trade not allocable	6,848	65	0.96
Total Finance, Insurance, and Real Estate	81,859	700	0.86
Banking	15,134	211	1.39
Credit Agencies other than Banks	9,881	182	1.84
Holding and Other Investment Companies	2,900	2	0.07

Appendix Table E-6 (continued)

	Total Compiled Receipts (in millions)	Advertising	Percent Relationship
Security and Commodity Brokers, Dealers, Exchanges, and Services	1,049	16	1.53
Insurance Carriers	39,901	101	0.25
Insurance Agents, Brokers, and Service	1,979	21	1.06
Real Estate except Lessors of Real Property other than Buildings	10,625	167	1.57
Lessors of Real Property except Buildings	390	*	0.05
Total Services	28,095	462	1.64
Hotels, Rooming Houses, Camps, and other Lodgings	3,248	74	2.28
Personal Services	3,478	57	1.64
Business Services	9,738	98	1.01
Automobile Repair, Services, & Garages, and other Repair Services	3,012	30	1.00
Motion Pictures	2,758	88	3.19
Amusement and Recreation Services except Motion Pictures	2,554	67	2.62
Other Services	3,307	46	1.39

* Less than $500,000: actual figures used to obtain percent relationship.

Source: U.S. Treasury Department, Internal Revenue Service, Statistics of Income—1962, Corporation Income Tax Returns, Washington, D.C., 1966, pp. 58-125.

Appendix Table E-7
Relative Importance of Advertising and Promotion for Leading Food Products, 1964 and Percent Change in Retail Prices and Wholesale Prices, 1947 and 1957-59 to 1965

	Retail Price	Advertising, Promotion	Advertising, Promotion to Retail Price (percent)	Retail Prices 1947 to 1965	Retail Prices 1957-59 to 1965	Wholesale Prices 1947 to 1965	Wholesale Prices 1957-59 to 1965
				(percent change)			
Breakfast cereals (1 lb.)	$ .416	$ .083	20.0	100.8	18.9	NA	NA
Canned corn, cream style (3 oz. can)	.190	.012	6.3	NA	NA	23.9	17.0
Evaporated milk (14-1/2 oz. can)	.149	.009*	6.0	21.0	5.3	11.7	1.2
Processed fruits and vegetables	100.00	6.00	6.0	15.4	7.3	9.3	2.1
Ice cream (1/2 gal.)	.804	.039	4.9	NA	-5.6	27.1	1.4
White bread (1 lb.)	.207	.010	4.8	78.4	14.7	76.3	9.5
Canned tomatoes (3 oz. can)	.160	.007	4.4	0	4.4	6.1	3.2
Cheese, American processed (1/2 lb.)	.367	.013	3.5	33.3	16.6	2.8	12.9
Fresh milk, in stores (1/2 gallon)	.477	.016	3.4	30.1	2.8	26.8	-8.7
Pork (pound)	.523	.018*	3.4	17.4	9.4	2.2	11.2

Appendix Table E-7 (continued)

	Retail Price	Advertising, Promotion	Advertising, Promotion Ratio to Retail Price	Retail Prices 1947 to 1965	Retail Prices 1957-59 to 1965	Wholesale Prices 1947 to 1965	Wholesale Prices 1957-59 to 1965
Veal (pound)	.781	.026*	3.3	-7.4	19.2	51.4	11.3
Broiler (pound)	.363	.012	3.3	-28.3	-9.7	57.5	-4.0
Eggs—grade B or better, all sizes(dozen)	.515	.017	3.3	-23.3	-7.2	-27.1	-6.5
Oranges, Florida (90 lb. box)	11.37	.370		84.7	18.4	42.4	-3.0
Turkey (pound)	.406	.012	3.0	NA	NA	NA	4.7
Butter (pound)	.744	.022	3.0	-2.9	3.6	-16.2	-1.5
Lamb, choice (pound)	.700	.021*	3.0	NA	NA	24.7	12.7
Beef, choice (pound)	.708	.020*	2.8	44.5	6.8	6.1	-8.8
Fresh milk, home delivery (1/2 gallon)	.528	.013	2.5	39.7	6.6	NA	NA
Apples, Washington delicious (42 lb. ctn.)	9.79	.240	2.5	52.7	19.7	12.8	6.4
Fresh fruits and vegetables		2.00	2.0	62.5	21.7	9.7	1.8
Total food index	100.00			33.8	8.8	15.4	5.1

N.A. not available

*Includes salesmen's salaries and brokerage.

Sources: National Commission on Food Marketing, *Food From Farmer to Consumer*, June 1966, pp. 16-17 and U.S. Department of Labor, Bureau of Labor Statistics.

Appendix Table E-8
Suggested Retail Prices of Selected
Proprietary Drugs, May 1939, 1947, and 1966

Product	Size	May 1939	1947	Early 1966
Noxzema	4 oz.	$ .50	.50	.75
Resinal Ointment	3-1/2 oz.	1.20	1.20	1.50
Zemo Liquid	8 oz.	1.00	1.00	1.65
Mentholatum	3 oz.	.60	.60	.98
Ben-Gay	1-1/4 oz.	.75	.75	.89
Musterole	2 oz.	.75	.75	1.09
Pertussin	8 oz.	1.00	1.00	1.29
Creomulsion	8 oz.	1.25	1.25	1.25
Creo-Terpin	3 oz.	.40	.50	.79
Anacin	100's	1.25	1.25	1.33
Bayer Aspirin	100's	.75	.75	.89
St. Joseph Aspirin	100's	.35	.35	.59
Phillips' Milk of Magnesia	12 oz.	.50	.50	.79
Feen-A-Mint	16's	.25	.25	.43
Listerine	7 oz.	.50	.50	.73
Astring-O-Sol	4 oz.	.60	.60	.65
Pepto-Bismol	4 oz.	.50	.50	.63
Bisodol	3 oz.	.65	.65	.89
TOTAL		12.80	12.90	17.12
Vaporub	1-1/2 oz.	NA	.35	.55
Fasteeth	4-1/4 oz.	NA	1.00	1.23
Alka-Seltzer	8's	NA	.30	.37
Sal Hepatica	6 oz.	NA	.60	.87
Fletcher's Castoria	2-1/2 oz.	NA	.40	.59
TOTAL			2.65	3.61
GRAND TOTAL			15.55	20.73

N.A. not available

Source: Drug Topics, Red Book—1939, 1946-47, and 1967.

Index